SURREALISM

Other books in the Eye on Art Series

SURREALISM

by Hal Marcovitz

LUCENT BOOKS
A part of Gale, Cengage Learning

GALE
CENGAGE Learning

Detroit • New York • San Francisco • New Haven, Conn • Waterville, Maine • London

GALE
CENGAGE Learning

Picture Credits

Cover, © Christie's Images/CORBIS, © C. Herscovici, Brussels/Artists Rights Society (ARS), New York; Banque d' Images, ADAGP/Art Resource, N.Y. © 2007 C. Herscovici, Brussels/Artists Rights Society (ARS), New York, 41; Digital Image © The Museum of Modern Art/Licensed by SCALA/Art Resource, N.Y. © 2007 Artists Rights Society (ARS), New York/ADAGP, Paris, 45; Digital Image © The Museum of Modern Art/Licensed by SCALA/Art Resource, N.Y. © 2007 Salvador Dali, Gala-Salvador Dali Foundation/Artists Rights Society (ARS), New York, 30; Digital Image © The Museum of Modern Art/Licensed by SCALA/Art Resource, N.Y. © 2007 The Pollock-Krasner Foundation/Artists Rights Society (ARS), New York, 51; Digital Image © The Museum of Modern Art/Licensed by SCALA/Art Resource, N.Y. Art © Estate of George Grosz/Licensed by VAGA, New York, NY., 66; Giraudon/Art Resource, N.Y., © 2007 Artist Rights Society (ARS), New York, ADAGP, Paris, 55, 69; Giraudon/Art Resource, N.Y. © 2007 Successio Miro/Artists Rights Society (ARS), New York/ADAGP, Paris, 71; Nimatallah/Art Resource, N.Y., © 2007 Estate of Pablo Picasso/Artist Rights Society (ARS), New York, 48; Phototheque R. Magritte/ADAGP/Art Resource, N.Y. © 2007 C. Herscovici, Brussels/Artist Rights Society (ARS), New York, 25; Snark/Art Resource, N.Y., 65; Tate, London/Art Resource, N.Y. © 2007 Artists Rights Society (ARS), New York/ADAGP, Paris, 23; © Albright-Knox Art Gallery/CORBIS, © Albright-Knox Art Gallery/CORBIS. © 2007 Successio Miro/Artists Rights Society (ARS), New York/ADAGP, Paris, 44; © Bettmann/CORBIS, 13; © Gero Breloer/epa/CORBIS, 89; © Francis G. Mayer/CORBIS, © 2007 Artists Rights Society (ARS), New York/ADAGP, Paris, 18; © Francis G. Mayer/CORBIS. © 2007 Salvador Dali, Gala-Salvador Dali Foundation/Artists Rights Society (ARS), New York, 35; © Condé Nast Archive/CORBIS, 17; © Photo B.D.V./CORBIS, 32; © Reuters/CORBIS, 61; © Alberto Ruggieri/Illustration Works/CORBIS, 92; © Stapleton Collection/CORBIS, © 2007 Man Ray Trust/Artists Rights Society (ARS), NY/ADAGP, Paris, 39; © Andy Warhol Foundation/CORBIS, © 2007 Andy Warhol Foundation for the Visual Arts/ARS, New York, 57; © Nogues Alain/CORBIS SYGMA, 77; © Pierre Vauthey/CORBIS SYGMA, 29; AFP/Getty Images, 84; Samantha Sin/AFP/Getty Images, © 2007 Estate of Pablo Picasso/Artists Rights Society (ARS), New York, 11; Roger Viollet/Getty Images, 20; Getty Images, 52; Lost Highway/CIBY 2000/The Kobal Collection/The Picture Desk, Inc., 80; Andre Paulve/Films Du Palais Royal/The Kobal Collection/Corbeau, Roger/The Picture Desk, Inc., 86; Universal/The Kobal Collection/The Picture Desk, Inc., 83

© 2008 Gale, a part of Cengage Learning

For more information, contact
Lucent Books
27500 Drake Rd.
Farmington Hills, MI 48331-3535
Or you can visit our Internet site at gale.cengage.com

LIBRARY OF CONGRESS CATALOGING-IN-PUBLICATION DATA

Marcovitz, Hal.
 Surrealism / by Hal Marcovitz.
   p. cm. — (Eye on art)
Includes bibliographical references and index.
ISBN-13: 978-1-4205-0005-9 (hardcover)
1. Surrealism—Juvenile literature. 2. Art, Modern—20th century—Juvenile literature. I. Title.
N6494.S8M333 2008
709.04'063—dc22
                                                          2007022930

Printed in the United States of America
3 4 5 6 7 12 11 10 09 08

CONTENTS

Foreword

"Art has no other purpose than to brush aside . . . everything that veils reality from us in order to bring us face to face with reality itself."

—French philosopher Henri-Louis Bergson

Some thirty-one thousand years ago, early humans painted strikingly sophisticated images of horses, bison, rhinoceroses, bears, and other animals on the walls of a cave in southern France. The meaning of these elaborate pictures is unknown, although some experts speculate that they held ceremonial significance. Regardless of their intended purpose, the Chauvet-Pont-d'Arc cave paintings represent some of the first known expressions of the artistic impulse.

From the Paleolithic era to the present day, human beings have continued to create works of visual art. Artists have developed painting, drawing, sculpture, engraving, and many other techniques to produce visual representations of landscapes, the human form, religious and historical events, and countless other subjects. The artistic impulse also finds expression in glass, jewelry, and new forms inspired by new technology. Indeed, judging by humanity's prolific artistic output throughout history, one must conclude that the compulsion to produce art is an inherent aspect of being human, and the results are among humanity's greatest cultural achievements: masterpieces such as the architectural marvels of ancient Greece, Michelangelo's perfectly rendered statue *David*, Vincent van Gogh's visionary painting *Starry Night*, and endless other treasures.

The creative impulse serves many purposes for society. At its most basic level, art is a form of entertainment or the means for a satisfying or pleasant aesthetic experience. But art's true power lies not in its potential to entertain and delight but in its ability to enlighten, to reveal the truth, and by doing so to uplift the human spirit and transform the human race.

One of the primary functions of art has been to serve religion. For most of Western history, for example, artists were paid by the church to produce works with religious themes and subjects. Art was thus a tool to help human beings transcend mundane, secular reality and achieve spiritual enlightenment. One of the best-known, and largest-scale, examples of Christian religious art is the Sistine Chapel in the Vatican in Rome. In 1508 Pope Julius II commissioned Italian Renaissance artist Michelangelo to paint the chapel's vaulted ceiling, an area of 640 square yards (535 sq. m). Michelangelo spent four years on scaffolding, his neck craned, creating a panoramic fresco of some three hundred human figures. His paintings depict Old Testament prophets and heroes, sibyls of Greek mythology, and nine scenes from the Book of Genesis, including the Creation of Adam, the Fall of Adam and Eve from the Garden of Eden, and the Flood. The ceiling of the Sistine Chapel is considered one of the greatest works of Western art and has inspired the awe of countless Christian pilgrims and other religious seekers. As eighteenth-century German poet and author Johann Wolfgang von Goethe wrote, "Until you have seen this Sistine Chapel, you can have no adequate conception of what man is capable of."

In addition to inspiring religious fervor, art can serve as a force for social change. Artists are among the visionaries of any culture. As such, they often perceive injustice and wrongdoing and confront others by reflecting what they see in their work. One classic example of art as social commentary was created in May 1937, during the brutal Spanish civil war. On May 1 Spanish artist Pablo Picasso learned of the recent attack on the small Basque village of Guernica by German airplanes allied with fascist forces led by Francisco Franco. The German pilots had used the village for target practice, a three-hour bombing that killed sixteen hundred civilians. Picasso, living in Paris, channeled his outrage over the massacre into his painting

Guernica, a black, white, and gray mural that depicts dismembered animals and fractured human figures whose faces are contorted in agonized expressions. Initially, critics and the public condemned the painting as an incoherent hodgepodge, but the work soon came to be seen as a powerful antiwar statement and remains an iconic symbol of the violence and terror that dominated world events during the remainder of the twentieth century.

The impulse to create art—whether painting animals with crude pigments on a cave wall, sculpting a human form from marble, or commemorating human tragedy in a mural—thus serves many purposes. It offers an entertaining diversion, nourishes the imagination and the spirit, decorates and beautifies the world, and chronicles the age. But underlying all these functions is the desire to reveal that which is obscure—to illuminate, clarify, and perhaps ennoble. As Picasso himself stated, "The purpose of art is washing the dust of daily life off our souls."

The Eye on Art series is intended to assist readers in understanding the various roles of art in society. Each volume offers an in-depth exploration of a major artistic movement, medium, figure, or profession. All books in the series are beautifully illustrated with full-color photographs and diagrams. Riveting narrative, clear technical explanation, informative sidebars, fully documented quotes, a bibliography, and a thorough index all provide excellent starting points for research and discussion. With these features, the Eye on Art series is a useful introduction to the world of art—a world that can offer both insight and inspiration.

Introduction

What Is
Surrealism?

Stony fingers hold aloft an egg with a flower growing through a crack in its shell. A man peers into a mirror to see the back of his own head. A soldier with the head of a bird wades through a war-torn landscape. A fish with a woman's legs reclines on a beach.

These are some of the most familiar images in surrealism, a movement in modern art that hit its pinnacle some seven decades ago. The surrealist images painted by such artists as Salvador Dalí, René Magritte, Max Ernst, Joan Miró, André Masson, Man Ray, and others have continued to startle, confound, and confuse art lovers for decades. They have also provided inspiration for generations of contemporary artists and filmmakers who have produced their own brand of surrealist art. Said Tim Martin, art history teacher at the University of Reading in England:

> To describe an event or experience as "surreal" today is to adopt a familiar figure of speech. The word immediately conjures up ideas of the weird and the wonderful, of disjointedness and disorientation, of the inexplicable

and the unfamiliar. We imagine worlds in which fish swim through the sky or inanimate objects metamorphose into living beings before our very eyes.[1]

Influenced by Freud

Surrealism is a word concocted in 1917 by the French poet Guillaume Apollinaire to describe a production of the ballet *Parade*. The ballet's producers had asked Apollinaire to write the text that appeared in the programs handed to audience members. It fell upon his shoulders to prepare the unsuspecting ballet lovers for the unusual performance that awaited them.

The ballet featured set designs and costumes by Spanish artist Pablo Picasso and the music of French composer Erik Satie. The ballet was light and whimsical, telling the story of circus performers and featuring jazzy music that was made by such unusual "instruments" as a typewriter, siren, pistol, and foghorn. The costumes and set designs were hardly what any-

Pablo Picasso's set design for the ballet *Parade* (shown) featured bold colors and whimsical characters.

one would expect to see on the ballet stage. Some of the costumes were made of cardboard, while the set designs, which depicted a nineteenth-century street carnival, reflected Picasso's interest in abstract art. To sum up this odd combination of the real and unreal, Apollinaire described the ballet as *surréalisme* or, in English, "super realism." Surrealism describes an image in which the unusual is depicted as a part of everyday life. However, true surrealism involves much more than just a visual image.

Surrealists were very influenced by Sigmund Freud, the founder of psychoanalysis, who suggested that humans are driven more by subconscious thoughts than conscious thoughts. Psychoanalysts such as Freud and Carl Jung suggested that the subconscious is a dark place that harbors inner drives, demons, frustrations, fears, and obsessions. Further, Jung believed that some universal thoughts are shared by all human minds, which explains how societies and cultures far removed from one another develop similar beliefs, rituals, and symbols. Jung suggested the subconscious holds the key to linking all human thought. In addition, Freud and Jung believed the subconscious remains active during sleep, manifesting itself in the form of dreams that often contain symbols. For example, a man who dreams his house has been robbed may, in his waking hours, be stealing from someone else. Perhaps his thefts are real: He may be helping himself to the cash register at his place of employment. Perhaps his thefts are not quite as obvious. He may simply be taking long lunch hours. Nevertheless, in his subconscious mind he believes he is stealing from his employer. His shame has manifested itself in the form of a dream in which he is the victim of a theft. In his 1900 book *The Interpretation of Dreams* Freud said, "If I dream I am frightened of robbers, the robbers are certainly imaginary, but the fear is real."[2]

Automatism

Surrealists strive to tap their subconscious to create art. However, subconscious thoughts are not easily mined. After all, they do not pop in and out of the artist's brain at will. Surrealists believe subconscious thoughts make themselves apparent during dreams or through "automatism," or free association, which was also a concept explored by Freud. To free-associate, a surrealist may observe a scene and then immediately apply the next thought that enters his or her mind to that image.

Jennifer Mundy, the senior curator at the Tate Gallery in London, said Freud helped the surrealists realize that they did not have to limit themselves to painting landscapes, portraits, and still life images that artists had been painting for centuries. Said Mundy:

> The Surrealists took from Freud confirmation of the existence of a deep reservoir of unknown and scarcely tapped energies within the psyche. Their use of techniques to reduce the element of conscious control in their drawings and writings, and their patient recording of dream imagery were more and more seen by the theorists of the movement as attempts to express the inner world of undirected and uncensored thought that Freud had described.[3]

Sigmund Freud (pictured) influenced the surrealists with his ideas about the subconscious.

Indeed, Freud once said, "The interpretation of dreams is the royal road to a knowledge of the unconscious activities of the mind."[4] Surrealists regarded that statement as a challenge to explore their dreams and free associations and create an outlet for their interpretations.

Scenes of Human Existence

Once they made it onto canvas, images from those dreams and free associations took on many strange shapes, colors, and concepts. Examples of surrealist art would include *The Man in the Bowler*

Hat, painted by Magritte, depicting a man wearing a bowler, but his face is obscured by a white dove flying by; or a painting by Ernst titled *The Elephant of Celebes*, which depicts a green mechanical elephant with the head of a bull. And then there is the most famous surrealist image ever painted: *The Persistence of Memory* by Dalí, which depicts the faces of watches melting in a barren, desertlike landscape.

All these images certainly depict unusual and even inexplicable events occurring in what are otherwise familiar scenes of human existence. What makes them truly surrealist is the artist's ability to mine the depths of his or her subconscious and transfer those thoughts to the canvas. By creating a surrealist image, the artist hopes to convey the universal experience of humankind in a symbolic way.

The Birth of Surrealism

The surrealist school of art was born shortly after World War I as a group of artists and intellectuals gathered in the coffee shops of Paris to try to make sense of the devastation that had just swept through Europe. The person who was often sitting at the center of these coffee shop discussions, providing the most influence on the early surrealist artists, was not an artist but a poet. André Breton, who worked in a French mental hospital during the war, had studied Freud and wondered whether the subconscious could be tapped as a source for literature. At first Breton was skeptical that the visual arts could become an outlet for surrealism, but when artists joined his movement and started producing works drawn from their subconscious thoughts, Breton became a proponent of the genre.

Many of the early surrealist artists had been working in other genres, including the abstract styles known as dadaism and cubism, both of which would influence surrealism. The early surrealists experimented with their styles, refining their work to fit into the rules of surrealism that Breton laid down in a manifesto he published in 1924. For much of the decade of the 1920s surrealist art would be confined to the galleries of

Paris, but late in the decade a flamboyant Spaniard, Salvador Dalí, joined the movement and helped spread surrealism to an international audience.

Dadaists and Cubists

During World War I dadaism emerged in Switzerland and soon spread throughout the European continent. (The French word *dada* means "hobby-horse." It was a whimsical expression picked for the name of the genre of art by two of its founders, Hugo Ball and Richard Huelsenbeck.) Like the surrealists, the dadaists wove unusual images into otherwise ordinary scenes. For example, French dadaist Marcel Duchamp mocked Leonardo da Vinci's masterpiece, the *Mona Lisa*, by painting a mustache and beard on the woman in the picture. Another early Duchamp depicts an upside-down men's room urinal. "Dada is the ground from which all art springs," French dadaist Jean Arp said. "Dada stands for art without sense. This does not mean nonsense. Dada is without a meaning, as Nature is."[5]

As Arp's words show, the dadaists had a generally comical outlook on life, and their art was certainly not drawn from any subconscious source. Still, surrealism owes something of a debt to dadaism, because the dadaists showed that art did not have to be limited to portraits, landscapes, still life scenes, and other familiar images but could be based on whatever weird and bizarre ideas an artist might conjure.

Another art form that would provide inspiration for surrealism is cubism. In cubism the artist dissects an image, breaks it down into tiny pieces, and then reassembles the images in an abstract form. Cubist portraits, such as those rendered by Picasso, often show hands, ears, heads, arms, and legs depicted out of place. When other objects are included in the scene, the painter is practicing a form of cubism known as synthetic cubism or collage cubism, after the French word for "paste-up." (Synthetic cubists often paste other materials—scraps of newspaper, swatches of cloth, discarded railroad tickets, trash from the wastepaper basket—right onto the canvas.) The artist

MARCEL DUCHAMP

The work of French dadaist Marcel Duchamp heavily influenced the early surrealists. Born into a family of artists in the French village of Blainville in 1887, Duchamp drew and painted in the classical style before embracing abstraction, particularly cubism.

His most famous work, which he painted in 1912, is *Nude Descending a Staircase, No. 2*. The cubist work was first displayed at the International Exhibition of Modern Art in New York City in 1913, in front of audiences who were unaccustomed to the weird abstract styles that dominated the French art community. Years later, the U.S. Postal Service issued a thirty-two-cent stamp depicting two puzzled art lovers studying Duchamp's painting.

Duchamp's urinal was among the works of Dada art he called "Readymades," which he defined as "everyday objects raised to the dignity of a work of art by the artist's act of choice." Among his other Readymades were a snow shovel, which he titled *In Advance of a Broken Arm*, and *Bicycle Wheel*, which he mounted on a wooden stool.

Duchamp created little art in his later years. He became an American citizen in 1955 and died in Paris in 1968.

Marcel Duchamp was drawn to cubism.

Quoted in Tim Martin, *Essential Surrealists*. Bath, UK: Dempsey Parr, 1999, p. 42.

given the most credit for developing synthetic cubism is Frenchman Georges Braque, whose 1913 painting *Still Life with Playing Cards* is regarded as a prime example of the genre. In the painting are drawings of cards from a deck as well as other images, such as a bunch of grapes, broken down into their most basic geometric shapes. Braque also included wood grains and other textures in the painting. Said Alfred H. Barr Jr., a former director of the Museum of Modern Art in New York, "In the *Still Life with Playing Cards* the geometrical shapes are so remotely related to the original form of the object that they seem almost to have been invented rather than derived. Their texture further adds to their independent reality so they may be considered not a breaking down or analysis, but a building up or synthesis."[6] Later, some surrealists would adopt the techniques of the cubists, breaking down objects and rearranging them into new shapes on the canvas or drawing in completely unassociated objects as part of the image.

In *Still Life with Playing Cards*, the artist breaks down a deck of cards and a bunch of grapes into their most basic geometric shapes.

The Rules of Surrealism

Some of the artists had to take a leave from dadaism and cubism to fight in World War I. Ernst served in the German army as an artilleryman. Masson, who fought in the French army, sustained a gunshot wound in the chest; the stretcher bearers were unable to remove him from the battlefield and were forced to leave him behind for the night. Miraculously, he survived. His biographer, Otto Hahn, suggested that Masson, gravely wounded and lying on his back, looked up at the stars and experienced his first surrealist inspiration. Wrote Hahn, "The world around him became something wondrous and he experienced his first complete physical release, while in the sky there appeared before him a torso of light."[7]

Breton also served in World War I. Stationed for a time as a medical orderly in a mental hospital in the town of Saint Dizier, Breton tended to the soldiers who had been driven insane on the battlefield. The patients he saw in the mental hospital did not speak with the voices of rational human beings. He saw physicians working with the patients, trying to unlock the tormented thoughts from their minds, often through hypnosis. Familiar with Freud's theories, Breton wondered whether subconscious thoughts could be articulated in literature. Later, in describing his experiences at Saint Dizier, Breton said, "The time I spent in this place, and the attention with which I studied what was happening have counted immensely in my life and have undoubtedly had a decisive influence on my manner of thinking."[8]

After the war other writers as well as many artists joined Breton in Paris's cafés, where the seeds of surrealism were sown. In 1920 Breton, with coauthor Philippe Soupault, published the novel *Les Champs Magnétiques* (in English, *The Magnetic Fields*), which is regarded as the first work of surrealist literature. In writing the book, Breton and Soupault broke numerous literary conventions. For example, they ended chapters at whatever point in the story they happened to be when they quit work for the day. The next morning they would pick up the story where they left off by starting a new chapter. In

ANDRÉ BRETON

Poet and novelist André Breton gave voice to the concept of surrealism. His *Manifesto of Surrealism* defined the movement and served as a guide for artists, writers, filmmakers, and other creative people who wished to employ surrealism in their work. Born in the Normandy region of France in 1896, Breton studied to be a physician but turned to writing after serving as a medical orderly in a mental institution during World War I.

Breton greatly admired nineteenth-century French poet Arthur Rimbaud, who was one of the originators of the French symbolist style of literature. To tell their stories, symbolists rely heavily on the use of symbols or metaphors rather than descriptions of real-life objects and experiences. Artists eventually adopted symbolist concepts as well. Certainly, the surrealists owe a debt to the symbolist movement.

Breton was also influenced by the writings of Karl Marx. He embraced socialism and encouraged other surrealists to adopt socialism as well, and many of them did follow Breton into the movement. Breton joined the French Communist party in 1927. In World War II he served in the French army but was expelled by the Nazi-backed Vichy government for his socialist activism. He fled to the United States and Canada, but after the war he returned to Paris, where he continued to support socialism and also made efforts to revive the surrealist movement. He died in 1966.

André Breton helped define surrealism.

writing the book, Breton and Soupault employed the technique of automatism—they let thoughts spill out of their brains onto the pages of the book, letting one word inspire the next. The fact that their sentences often made no sense did not discourage them from completing their manuscript. One of the book's sentences reads: "Do not disturb the genius planter of white roots my nerve endings underground."[9] While critics debated the value of surrealist literature, Breton and the other surrealists pressed on.

In 1924 the rules and concepts of surrealism were drawn up by Breton, who issued his *Manifesto of Surrealism*. He defined surrealism as

> psychic automatism in its pure state, by which one proposes to express—verbally, by means of the written word, or in any other manner—the actual functioning of thought. Dictated by thought, in the absence of any control exercised by reason, exempt from any aesthetic or moral concern.
>
> Surrealism is based on the belief in the superior reality of certain forms of previously neglected associations, in the omnipotence of dreams, in the disinterested play of thought. It tends to ruin once and for all other psychic mechanisms and to substitute itself for them in solving all the principal problems of life.[10]

Breton intended surrealism to provide new rules for literature. At first he rejected visual art as an outlet for surrealism but eventually came to believe surrealism could be the basis for any type of artistic expression. In fact, elsewhere in the manifesto he talked about a dream in which he envisioned a man, who had been sliced in two, standing at his window. Clearly, he appreciated the artistic possibilities inherent in such a vision. Describing the image of the severed man in his dream, Breton said,

> There could be no question of ambiguity, accompanied as it was by the faint visual image. (Were I a painter,

this visual depiction would doubtless have become more important for me. . . .) Since that day, I have had occasion to concentrate my attention voluntarily on similar apparitions, and I know they are fully as clear as auditory phenomena. With a pencil and white sheet of paper in hand, I could easily trace their outlines.[11]

Colorful Time in Paris

It did not take long for artists to be drawn to the surrealist movement. In 1925 the first major exhibition of surrealist art was displayed at the Galerie Pierre in Paris, which featured the work of Masson and Miró as well as Man Ray, an artist-photographer whose real name was Emmanuel Radnitzky. Born in Philadelphia, Radnitzky adopted the name Man Ray by shortening his nickname, Manny, into "Man," and then shortening his last name into "Ray." Man Ray first experimented with dadaism after meeting Duchamp in New York; in 1921 he moved to Paris and embraced surrealism. Man Ray was predominantly a painter, but he would soon experiment with photography. In 1926 Galerie Surréaliste, a gallery in Paris devoted entirely to surrealism, opened with an exhibition of Man Ray's art.

This was a vibrant, exciting, and colorful time to be an artist in Paris. Following the war, creative people from many walks of life converged on the French capital, taking up residence in the hip district known as the Left Bank. Many were American writers, including Ernest Hemingway, Gertrude Stein, Ezra Pound, and F. Scott Fitzgerald. They spent their afternoons in cafés or in each other's tiny flats, playing cards, sipping wine, and discussing art, jazz, literature, and politics. In the evenings the Left Bank denizens made the rounds of the city's bistros. In between the drinking, card-playing, and leisurely strolls along the Champs-Elysées, books were written, music was composed, and paintings were created. Indeed, all of the arts were heading in new directions. The surrealists were a part of this community, and there is no question that they were among the most creative artists to emerge from Paris in the 1920s.

The early paintings by the surrealists show how they absorbed Breton's pronouncements about surrealism and adopted it into their work. Ernst clearly got the idea. He painted *The Elephant of Celebes* in 1921, rendering the lumbering beast against a desertlike background—with a few fish swimming across the sky—while a headless nude bids the elephant to follow her. Art historian Uwe M. Schneede suggested that *The Elephant of Celebes* is a clear example of how surrealists sought to merge the unreal with the real. Schneede said the objects in the picture are unreal, but Ernst painted them with such clarity and precision that the impression he leaves is one of make-believe objects existing in the real world. Said Schneede, "In the artificial world of the picture, things that do not exist elsewhere become real. The picture constitutes an anti-world of fantasy and the psychic implications of such a world."[12]

Masson's early surrealist work employed elements of cubism. The artist's *Underground Figure*, painted in 1924, shows a bald-headed nude unfurling a scroll. In the background are vague representations of a bird, the sun, a bottle on a shelf, and an hourglass. He used few colors in his early surrealist paintings, preferring to give the images a flat, muted look of grays and subtle red and purple tones. (In later years the surrealist movement would be known for its vivid use of bright, incandescent colors.) Martin said the painting helped lay the groundwork for Masson's later work because it was one of his first paintings to employ symbolism, in which Masson used simple objects to represent much more complex thoughts. In the painting, Martin said, man dominates the objects depicted by Masson, just as he dominates his own universe. "Elements of symbolism make this work an important stage in the formation of Masson's more wholly Surrealist paintings."[13]

Miró's 1924 painting *The Gentleman* depicts a very colorful foot providing the lone support for a stick figure who sports a mustache and a shock of red hair that resembles the feathers of a rooster. The figure is painted on a green background. According to Carolyn Lanchner, curator of paintings and sculpture at the Museum of Modern Art in New York, *The Gentleman* represents a blurring of the lines between the real and the musings of Miró's subconscious. "Miró's fancifully outfitted gentleman delivers poetry by way of humor," said Lanchner. "Whatever the picture's source may have been, a fluid ambivalence between physical and mental events is realized."[14]

The Gentleman, like most of Miró's work, was a product of automatism. "I do not start with the idea that I will paint a certain thing," Miró insisted. "I start to paint and while I am painting the picture begins to take effect, it reveals itself. In the act of painting, a shape will begin to mean woman, or bird."[15]

The Arrival of Dalí

The late 1920s marked a major explosion in surrealist art. In the beginning the movement had been limited to the Parisian galleries, but by the latter years of the decade artists from other countries had been drawn to the movement, and soon surrealist art would receive international exposure. As new artists started exploring surrealism, they brought distinctive styles to the craft. For example, Magritte, a Belgian, painted one of his first surrealist images, *Le Jockey Perdu* (in English, *The Lost Jockey*), in 1926. The painting depicts a man riding a horse through a landscape of trees that resemble marble columns decorated with bars of music; in the foreground, curtains are drawn back to reveal the scene. A.M. Hammacher, a German art critic and former museum director, said Magritte intended the bars of music to dominate the image, hence making the jockey lost in the world of the painting. He said, "The bars of music contribute rhythmical transparency to the picture, in which the jockey becomes lost as though in some enchanted domain."[16]

René Magritte's *Le Jockey Perdu* brought a distinctive style to surrealist painting.

Jean Cocteau and the Ox on the Roof

During the 1920s the surrealists met in Parisian cafés where they talked about their art and inspirations. The one café in Paris where they were most likely to meet was Le Boeuf sur le Toit, which in English means "The Ox on the Roof."

The café's owner borrowed the name for his eatery from the title of a ballet directed by French surrealist Jean Cocteau. Cocteau was also the director of the ballet *Parade*, the production of which prompted poet Guillaume Apollinaire to first use the word "surréalisme."

Cocteau would regularly hold court in the café, dining with his friend André Breton and other leading surrealists. Cocteau was often joined by the American artist and photographer Man Ray as well as other artists of the surrealist movement, including Salvador Dalí. Later, Cocteau was one of surrealism's most successful film directors. His most famous film was *Beauty and the Beast*, which he directed in 1946. The film includes such surrealist images as disembodied hands holding candle sticks, doors magically opening, and statues coming to life. "Cocteau's film is poetry in motion," said film critic Toni Ruberto, "a sumptuous visual feast that brought a fantasy world to life with a surreal and exquisite touch. One of its most memorable scenes has Belle's loving tears turn to diamonds."

Cocteau died in 1963 at the age of seventy-four. As for Le Boeuf sur le Toit, it is still in business in Paris and is a gourmet French restaurant.

Toni Ruberto, "The Beauty in the Beast: Tales of the Deformed and Unloved Are Some of the Most Romantic Ever Told," *Buffalo News*, February 11, 2007.

Magritte also had a taste for the grotesque. His 1926 painting *The Menaced Assassin* depicts a man listening to a gramophone while the nude and bloody body of a female corpse lies nearby. Standing behind two walls, ready to bludgeon the killer with a club and capture him in a net, are two other men. Meanwhile, three men peer in through a window, standing in front of a background of snow-capped mountains. Evidently, Magritte was influenced by more than his subconscious thoughts. He enjoyed reading detective stories—he even tried writing some himself—and appreciated the dark poetry of Edgar Allen Poe. Schneede said *The Menaced Assassin* represents a technique practiced by many surrealists: taking a simple story—in this case, a murder—and turning it into a rather elaborate scenario:

> If we accept the picture's invitation to guess at what has gone before and what will happen next, we reach this conclusion: a murderer is spending a moment listening to beautiful music while his captors stand ready to apprehend him. There is no escape, because the window, too, has been blocked. To find so trivial a story worthy of art is typical for a Surrealist.[17]

In addition to Magritte, others drawn to the surrealist school in Paris were Germans Richard Oelze and Méret Oppenheim, Rumanians Victor Brauner and Jacques Hérold, and the Swiss painters Kurt Seligman and Alberto Giacometti. Also making their way to Paris were Hans Bellmer, a Pole; Wolfgang Paalen, an Austrian; Oscar Dominguez, a Spaniard; Marie Cermínová, a Czech who painted under the name of Toyen; Enrico Donati, an Italian; and Grégoire Michonze, a Russian. Man Ray remained America's leading surrealist of the era.

The fact that artists with an interest in surrealism were flocking to Paris showed how much of an impact the movement had made on the international art community in the handful of years since Breton published his manifesto. Soon the appeal of surrealism would explode even further, captivating audiences across the globe.

In 1928 a flamboyant Spaniard joined the movement and would be instrumental in turning surrealism into a major school of art. He was a classically trained painter, although he experimented with a number of abstract styles. Kicked out of art school for his political activism and eccentric behavior but mostly for showing contempt to his teachers—he did not believe them capable of teaching him—Salvador Dalí moved to Paris at the urging of Miró, whom he had met in Madrid. When he arrived, Miró introduced him to the city's most influential surrealist artists. Dalí was drawn into their circle and soon started painting his own surrealist images.

The Persistence of Memory

He completed his first surrealist painting, *The First Day of Spring*, in 1929. It provided the benchmark for a career in surrealism that would span the next five decades. The painting shows a blue sky glistening over a gray landscape populated by various characters—a man sitting in a chair, a little girl confronting an older man, a fish, a nude, a bird's head in a box, a man walking a dog, a baby's picture in a frame, an abstract painting within the painting, an upside-down grasshopper, and other images. The French surrealist community was immediately smitten by the Spaniard's talent. Said surrealist poet Robert Desnos, "It's like nothing that is being done in Paris."[18] As for Dalí, he had no doubt that he belonged in the surrealist school and, in fact, fully intended to emerge as the leader of the movement. He said,

> Although I plunged into the craziest ventures with the same eagerness as they, I was already laying—with Macchiavellian skepticism—the structural foundation for the next step in the eternal tradition. The Surrealists seemed the only ones who formed a group whose methods would serve my plans. Their leader, André Breton, seemed irreplaceable in his function as visible head of the movement. As for me, I tried to lead, but by means of a secret influence, both opportunistic and contradictory.[19]

Dalí was eccentric. He once gave a lecture at the French university La Sorbonne with his foot submerged in a pail of milk and showed up at a press conference wearing a lobster on his head. When he signed an autograph he always kept the pen. He was also very likely to have suffered from mental illness. He told friends that he feared being devoured alive. Dalí hallucinated and often fell into fits of uncontrollable laughter. He selected weird and wordy titles for his paintings. Among his wordiest titles were *Skull with Its Lyric Appendage Leaning on a Night Table Which Should Have the Exact Temperature of a Cardinal Bird's Nest* and *Gala Contemplating the Mediterranean Sea Which at Twenty Meters Becomes the Portrait of Abraham Lincoln (Homage to Rothko)*.

Nevertheless, his talent was unquestioned. Soon after completing *The First Day of Spring*, he painted *Illuminated Pleasures*. The painting featured a variety of human and animal faces, a self-portrait, a pattern of bicyclists, a hand holding a bloody dagger, and a woman splashing waves against a cliff. Clearly, he drew those images from his subconscious.

A renowned eccentric, Salvador Dalí lives up to expectations at a 1979 press conference.

The strange images in *The Persistence of Memory* gave surrealism a boost in the international art world.

In 1931 he painted *The Persistence of Memory*, the painting most responsible for setting the tone for his own work and boosting surrealism into an international phenomenon. The painting features the faces of watches melting against a barren landscape. The weirdness of *The Persistence of Memory*, along with Dalí's eccentricities, his flamboyance, and his talent at self-promotion, helped catapult surrealism onto the international stage. Suddenly, art critics, art collectors, gallery owners, museum curators, and other important people in the art world took notice of this bizarre form of art, which was strange even by abstract standards. In fact, in 1936 Dalí was featured on the cover of *Time* magazine. The surrealists had now been given a place in the public consciousness ordinarily reserved for statesmen, scientists, and sports heroes.

The Surrealists

The early surrealist artists experimented with styles and materials, each bringing important contributions to the genre. Their innovations ranged from tinkering with their paints, canvases, and other materials to much more outlandish and bizarre notions such as starving themselves or depriving themselves of sleep in order to further probe the secrets of their subconscious thoughts.

The most common theme they maintained in their art, however, was the merger of the real with the unreal, which had been an integral part of surrealism since the dancers first took the stage in the ballet *Parade*. Salvador Dalí had his own term for it. He called it "concrete irrationality."[20] He said, "My whole ambition in the pictorial domain is to materialize the images of concrete irrationality. . . . In order that the world of the imagination and of concrete irrationality may be as objectively evident, of the same consistency, of the same durability, of the same persuasive and communicable thickness as that of the exterior world of phenomenal reality."[21]

There is no question that the surrealists were innovators. Although they took inspiration from the dadaists, the cubists, and other abstract artists, their work was unique in many

DALÍ'S MUSE

Many of Salvador Dalí's paintings include the image of the same woman. It is his wife, Gala, to whom he was devoted from the time of their marriage in 1932 until her death fifty years later.

She was born Helena Diakanoff Devulina in Russia to wealthy parents. In 1913, at the age of nineteen, her family sent her to a hospital in Switzerland for treatment of tuberculosis. While undergoing treatment she met French poet Paul Éluard. Eventually she married Éluard and moved to Paris with him, where she adopted the name Gala. In 1929 she met Dalí, and three years later divorced Éluard to marry the Spanish painter.

Theirs was a most unusual marriage. She had many romantic affairs, which Dalí did not mind and may even have encouraged. Dalí was flamboyant, eccentric, and a talented artist, but he knew nothing about business. Gala took over his business affairs, managed his career, and made her husband extremely wealthy.

She died in 1982, seven years before Dalí. He was heartbroken and told his friends there was no reason to go on living. For the final years of his life he lived as a virtual shut-in. Mired in depression and suffering from Parkinson's disease, he painted little, starved himself, and virtually withered away until he died. He gave his final surrealist drawing, which he titled *Head of Europa*, to King Juan Carlos of Spain as a gift. He made the drawing on his deathbed.

Gala and Salvador Dalí appear in public two years before her death.

ways. As the first members of the school they had founded, the surrealists set the tone for a style of art that would endure for decades.

Trained as an Impressionist

Before embracing surrealism, Dalí had been trained in the classic style of painting known as impressionism. Impressionists paint brightly lit images showing vivid colors and broad brush strokes. The impressionists often let their brush strokes bleed over the lines. They were also among the first artists to take their easels outdoors. They believed that painting *en plein air*, a French expression that means "in the open air," gave them the opportunity to capture colors in their most natural forms.

Dalí was born in 1904 in the Spanish town of Figueras in the region of Spain known as Catalonia. Figueras is near Spain's Costa Brava along the Mediterranean Sea. All his life Dalí was awestruck by the beauty of the Costa Brava and, as a young boy, painted many scenes of the Spanish landscape near his home.

As a child he was surrounded by doting women—his mother, sisters, aunts, grandmother, and a nurse—who spoiled him. He grew up wild and rebellious but also craved isolation and spent hours by himself.

His childhood was strange and tortured. Dalí's older brother, also named Salvador, died at the age of two before Salvador was born. The loss of the boy caused his parents to feel grief for years; they kept a portrait of the young child on the wall in their bedroom. As for Salvador, he was haunted by the image of his brother his whole life, believing that his parents conceived him as a replacement for the first Salvador. He once said, "All the eccentricities I commit, I do because I wish to prove to myself that I am not the dead brother, but the living one."[22]

Dalí staged the first exhibition of his paintings at the age of fourteen. Four years later he enrolled in the Royal Academy of Fine Arts of San Fernando in Madrid. It was Spain's top art school.

He was quickly recognized as the school's top student, but by now he had started to experiment with abstraction. He was impressed with the cubist paintings of Picasso, whose style he wanted to imitate. This angered his teachers who insisted that he concentrate on impressionism. Dalí, who had long been interested in the meaning of his own dreams, started reading books by Sigmund Freud. He also started espousing socialist politics.

At the Royal Academy Dalí bristled under the authority of his teachers and concluded that they could teach him nothing. In 1923 the school's administrators found an excuse to suspend him. To break up a student protest the school identified Dalí as a ringleader and kicked him out for a year. Returning home, he was briefly imprisoned for his socialist activities. Back in Madrid following his suspension, Dalí studied at the Royal Academy for another two years. He continued to experiment with abstract styles and fight with his teachers. Finally, in late 1926 at the age of twenty-two, he was kicked out for good.

Photographic Clarity

Dalí maintained a caustic relationship with his teachers at the Royal Academy, but there is no question that he honed his skills as a stylist under their instruction. Indeed, one of Dalí's most important contributions to surrealism is his work as a stylist: His paintings are very intricate; in his work, the tiniest details are painted in photographic clarity. The influence of impressionism can be found in his use of bright colors. The Costa Brava landscapes he painted as a boy show up often in the backgrounds of his surrealist paintings.

Dalí's paintings include many of the fundamental aspects of surrealist art. For example, he linked objects that would appear to have no association with one another into a single image. Also, Dalí often depicted objects performing functions that they do not normally perform. In the *Metamorphosis of Narcissus*, which Dalí painted in 1937, he depicted a flower growing out of a cracked egg; in his 1938 painting *Apparition of Face and Fruit Dish on a Beach* a man's head is employed as a fruit bowl, and in *The Burning Giraffe*, from 1937, he painted a woman's torso and leg as a chest of drawers. These were only some of the images that Dalí rendered in those paintings; each painting included many more images, most intertwined with one another, often providing a challenge to the eye to try to make sense of the action. In *Apparition of Face and Fruit Dish on a Beach*, a close inspection of the painting reveals that not only is the fruit dish turned into the face, but the chin, lips, and nose of the face form the back of a sitting woman. Said British art historian Paul Moorehouse, "In these works Dalí pushed the phenomenon of images within images further than either he or [surrealism's] earlier exponents had achieved. . . . In *Apparition of Face and Fruit Dish on a Beach* the complexity of image challenges the observer to decode its matrix of hidden appearances. . . . The bowl of fruit becomes a face, the face becomes a seated woman. . . . Dalí's mastery in simultaneously asserting and denying appearances is reflected in this work."[23]

Dalí's *Apparition of Face and Fruit Dish on a Beach* challenges the viewer's ability to see multiple images.

DALÍ ATOMICUS

There is a famous photograph of Salvador Dalí that features an image of the Spanish artist, paintbrush in hand, floating in the air while an easel floats nearby. The photograph also includes a chair and a bucket of water tossed through the air as well as three cats flying by. The photograph, titled *Dalí Atomicus*, was taken in 1948 by photographer Philippe Halsman. The title of the photograph was based on one of Dalí's paintings, *Leda Atomica*, which floats in the photo as well.

The photograph was taken decades before the invention of digital photography, meaning that there was no manipulation of the image on a computer. Dalí had to leap for the camera while the cats and water were tossed across the viewfinder as well. It took six hours and twenty-eight tries before Halsman was satisfied with the image caught by his camera. Eventually, the photograph was featured in *Life* magazine.

Said Halsman, "Dalí was known for his antics, without needing the help of my camera. I called him and said I'd like to make a photograph that I would call *Dalí Atomicus*, in which everything would be suspended. The easel would be in mid-air, Dalí would be in mid-air, and even the subject of the painting would be in suspension. Dalí thought it a marvelous idea, I was invited over to discuss the details."

Quoted in Joanna Pitman, "Salvador Dalí in Mid-Air," the *Times*, May 8, 2004.

The watch faces in his 1931 painting *The Persistence of Memory* challenge the viewer to find a purpose in the images other than the telling of time. In fact, the watch faces are not intended to tell time, but instead they suggest the universe is timeless and has no clock. In the background of the painting, Dalí has painted the rocky cliffs of Cadaqués on the Costa Brava. Art critic Robert Goff suggested that Dalí placed the cliffs in the background to show that they would remain standing for thousands of years. "In the Dalían universe, soft objects are detestable: They are powerless and putrefying," said Goff. "Only hard objects, such as the rocks of Cadaqués in the background, have worth: Time has no power over them."[24]

Away from the canvas Dalí craved the attention of the press, which helped shed light on the surrealist movement. His desire for fame and wealth made him no friends among other surrealists who accused him of being more interested in money than in furthering the goals of surrealist art. In 1934, after Dalí accepted a commission to provide surrealist paintings to advertise a company that manufactured women's stockings, Breton declared Dalí a traitor to the movement. Breton and the other surrealists believed their art should not be commercialized. To insult the artist, Breton rearranged the letters in Salvador Dalí's name into the term "*avida* dollars," which translates roughly into "eager for dollars."[25] Dalí shot back, "The only difference between me and the Surrealists is that I am a Surrealist."[26] The schism between Dalí and the other surrealists would never heal; until the ends of their lives Breton and the others regarded Dalí as an outcast.

Surrealist from Philadelphia

While Dalí was born into the European privileged class, Man Ray was raised among far more modest means. Born in 1890 in Philadelphia to Russian immigrants, Man Ray's father was a tailor. As a child Emmanuel was surrounded by needles, flatirons, fabric, mannequins, and spools of thread. In later years these objects would dominate his artwork. His 1921 dadaist photograph, *Cadeau* (in English, *Gift*) shows a common flatiron, albeit with fourteen spikes protruding from the surface that would otherwise come into contact with the article of clothing to be ironed.

Man Ray's artistic talent blossomed while he attended high school in New York, where his family opened a tailor shop when Emmanuel was seven years old. His talent in his high school mechanical drawing and lettering classes prompted New York University to offer him a scholarship to study architecture, but he turned it down because he desired to be a painter. After high school he supported himself as a commercial artist and took lessons in fine art when he could afford them.

In 1915 the Daniel Gallery in New York staged an exhibition of his work. He also met Duchamp that year. Duchamp introduced Man Ray to dadaism, and soon he was creating art in that style. His 1920 sculpture *New York* depicts a tall bottle filled with steel ball bearings. The piece is similar to Duchamp's "Readymades"—ordinary objects that the artist chooses to recognize as art. New York art curator Ingrid Schaffner said Man Ray's work from this period challenged people to look beyond the physical object he employed in the sculpture and appreciate the piece for the idea it means to convey. She said, "Using everyday items, often mass produced, Man Ray created objects, like *New York*, a glass bottle of ball bearings, that captured the tension of working and living bottled up in a landscape of skyscrapers. These objects related to Duchamp's Readymades by shifting attention from the art object to the ideas that transform it into a work of art."[27]

Gallery owners, art critics, and collectors were not yet sold on Dada, and Man Ray found it difficult to generate interest in his work. In 1921 Man Ray declared, "Dada cannot live in New York. All New York is Dada, and will not tolerate a rival."[28] He left that year for Paris and soon found himself drawn into the surrealist movement.

Man Ray's paintings display some familiar surrealist themes—his 1934 painting *L'Heure de L'Observatoire—Les Amoureux* (in English, *Observatory Time—The Lovers*) depicts a woman's rouged lips floating across a cloudy sky, while below, a nude reclines alongside a chess board. Perhaps his most famous painting, which he rendered in 1938, is *Portrait of the Marquis de Sade*. Man Ray's study of the famous French nobleman—whose place in history was earned through his strange sexual practices—features the marquis constructed of bricks, watching stone-faced as a mob attacks and sets fire to the Bastille, France's notorious prison. French art historian Marina Vanci-Perahim said the painting and others are significant additions to surrealist art because they add a three-dimensional perspective to the genre. For example, she said, in *Portrait of the Marquis de Sade*, Man Ray has painted the brickwork curving around the face. "No longer reducing his images to two dimensions, he developed an illusionist pictorial space that was better adapted to his dreamscapes."[29]

In *Portrait of the Marquis de Sade*, Man Ray introduced three-dimensional perspective.

Solarization and Rayographs

Man Ray was an important surrealist painter, but it is as a photographer that the artist expanded surrealism into other genres of creativity. *Le Violon d'Ingres* (in English, *The Violin of Ingres*) is one of Man Ray's most famous photographs. Produced in 1924, it depicts facsimiles of F holes—the curvy slots found on the face of a stringed instrument—inked onto the naked back of a woman.

Man Ray also employed the solarization process in surrealist photography. The technique is produced in the darkroom by giving prints under development a second exposure to light. If done properly, the technique results in a fuzzy black halo around the object in the photo, giving the image a dreamy quality that helps add to the surreal feeling of the photograph.

Another surrealist style Man Ray brought to photography could be found in his "Rayographs." These were photographs made by placing ordinary household objects onto photographic paper, then exposing them to light. After the prints were developed, they depicted eerie silhouettes of the objects. Among his Rayograph images are depictions of keys, pistols, human profiles, and sewing needles. According to Schaffner, Man Ray's skill at solarization as well as his development of the Rayograph show that the artist found a way to merge the real with the unreal. Said Schaffner, "Surrealist photography exploited our basic assumption that photography presented reality as we 'saw' it and then shocked us by going beyond that reality, or by undermining it."[30]

Supper at Home

Where Dalí was flamboyant and Man Ray a willing denizen of the Parisian café community, Magritte was quiet and reserved and preferred to have supper at home with his family. As Dalí sought wealth and fame, Magritte preferred to live the life more familiar to middle-class working people. He painted in his own home, setting up his easel in his dining room.

His 1958 painting *Golconde* (in English, *Golconda*, which is the name of a former fortress city in India) is a self-portrait.

The painting shows Magritte in numerous duplications of himself, dressed in suit and bowler hat, raining down on a cityscape. British art historian David Sylvester said that in *Golconde*, Magritte makes a statement about the inability of individuals to assert themselves in a cluttered society. "They seem stuck there in space like repetitions of an ornamental device," Sylvester said of the many replications of Magritte in the painting. "In fact they are parts of a pattern like a wallpaper pattern, infinitely repeatable and extendable. They seem a sample of an infinity of identically helpless beings."[31]

Magritte's paintings also show the whimsical side of surrealism. His 1937 painting *Portrait of Edward James* depicts his model looking into a mirror to see the back of his own head— the same image the viewer sees as he or she examines the painting. His 1934 painting *Collective Invention* depicts a fish crawling out of the ocean, its tail fins replaced by a woman's legs. It is the opposite of the classic image of the mermaid. It is a humorous image, but some critics have suggested it shows

While looking into a mirror, a model sees the back of his head rather than the front in *Portrait of Edward James.*

that Magritte did have a darker side. Art historian Bradley Collins Jr. said Magritte may have drawn the image from his childhood, when he saw the body of his mother wash up on the river's edge. His mother, Regina Magritte, committed suicide by throwing herself into a river. "In *Collective Invention*, which turns a woman into a fish from the waist up, he alludes to his mother's drowned body," said Collins, "and [he] mocks her—by jumping into the river she has become no better than a fish."[32]

Rubbing the Floorboards

Ernst made the transition from dadaism to surrealism. His 1919 Dada painting *The Master's Bedroom It's Worth Spending a Night There* shows various animals—a snake, miniature whale, bat, fish, bear, and lamb—occupying a bedroom, although their human owner is not in the picture. The lack of the human prompts the viewer to wonder whether it truly is worth spending the night. Spanish art historian José María Faerna said the artist's use of perspective in the painting, which depicts wide spaces between the furniture and the animals, makes it even less inviting to the visitor. "The sense of unreality is ominously heightened by the extreme rendering of perspective and by the precarious placement of the furniture,"[33] he said.

By 1921 Ernst left dadaism to concentrate on surrealism. That was the year he painted *The Elephant of Celebes*. Like Man Ray, Ernst looked for new ways to use the tools and materials of the artist. He helped develop a technique known as frottage, which involves making rubbings of textured surfaces, which are then transferred to the canvas.

Ernst discovered the frottage method one evening when he stopped at an inn and noticed the rough, textured surface of the floorboards. Ernst dropped sheets of paper onto the floor, fell to his knees, and rubbed the surface with a pencil. He was awestruck by the patterns that emerged from the rubbings and soon incorporated them into his work.

He also perfected the technique known as decalcomania, which added a dreamy, mystical atmosphere to his paintings.

Decalcomania involves painting on glass, then pressing the glass onto canvas. Ernst believed that transferring the paintings in this way helped make them more abstract and gave him a better insight into the images he believed were alive in his subconscious. His painting *Day and Night*, which he completed in 1942, was produced through the decalcomania process and shows a number of intricately painted pylons rising from what appears to be a prehistoric landscape. Various parts of the painting are rendered in bright colors, signifying day, while others are painted in dim shades, signifying night.

Day and Night was painted as war raged in Europe. Ernst had been displaced by the war—he had been imprisoned for a time by the Nazis, then released. Forced to sneak out of Europe, Ernst made his way to America and painted *Day and Night* shortly after arriving. Art historian John Russell suggested that *Day and Night* depicts Ernst's attempt to remain in control of his life and art, regardless of what was happening in Europe. "His determination to get these opposites and antitheses into one and the same picture may have resulted, I think, from a determination to not be overwhelmed by the paradoxes and contradictions of wartime life," said Russell. "Somehow, the artist had to be the master of them . . . he must rise above whatever was put in his way."[34]

Depriving Themselves of Sleep

Dalí's mentor, Miró, was one of the founders of the surrealist movement, but he resisted that description for his work, believing himself free to work in a number of styles. Still, Miró sought to probe his subconscious in search of surrealist images. To find these images Miró attempted to induce a hallucinogenic state by starving himself and depriving himself of sleep. His most famous work, *Harlequin's Carnival*, was conceived while Miró was under the influence of sleep deprivation. The painting, which Miró produced in 1925, includes dozens of images such as streamers blowing in the wind, masks, cats, guitars, mustaches, fish, winged creatures, and other shapes that Miró believed he had drawn from his subconscious mind.

The fanciful images in Miró's *Harlequin's Carnival* resulted after the artist deprived himself of sleep.

French art historian Jacques Lassaigne said *Harlequin's Carnival* is populated by many diverse images but nevertheless is held together by a number of visual techniques Miró employed in the painting. He said,

> Extremely complex but never overloaded, the composition is built up quite straightforwardly around the central figure, a man playing a guitar. The wire-drawn axis of his body, duplicated by a white spiral, bisects the canvas vertically, and is divided horizontally by the line formed by the junction of the floor and wall, and also by an arm ending in a monstrous hand. This intersection, though twice repeated, is not pronounced enough to disturb the overall balance, but acts on the contrary as a unifying factor.[35]

In the painting, the figure of Harlequin—a clown who first appeared in fifteenth-century Italian comic theater—can be found in the upper left-hand corner of the painting. Lassaigne suggested that Miró painted Harlequin as a self-portrait. "He represents . . . Miró himself," said Lassaigne, "watcher and donor of this strange masterwork."[36]

Another artist who experimented with sleep deprivation was Masson, who brought a cubist influence to surrealism and mostly employed automatism in creating his work. He also denied himself nourishment, hoping to enter a trance so that he could probe his subconscious. Like other surrealists, he experimented with techniques and materials—he often coated his canvases with glue and then threw sand onto them, finally painting on top of the shapes that were formed. Masson believed the artist should not be able to control the surface on which he or she painted—that was why the sand was tossed on at random.

One of his most famous "sand pictures" is titled *Battle of Fish*, which he completed in 1927. Painted through automatism while Masson was in a sleep-deprived trance, the picture shows various line drawings of fish attacking one another. Virtually the only color in the painting is represented through

André Masson created unusual painting surfaces by coating his canvases with glue and covering them with sand, as he did in *Battle of Fish* (pictured).

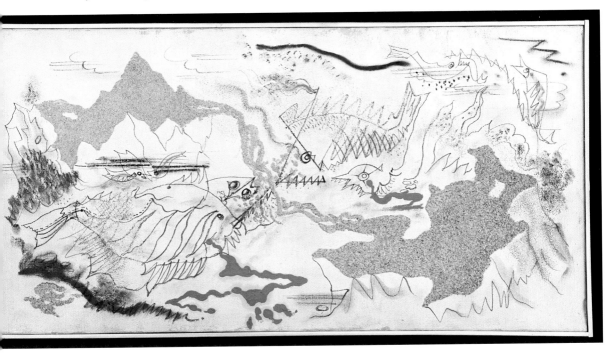

blobs of red paint—symbolizing blood—while the sand has taken on the look of a mountain, suggesting that the fish were not necessarily fighting underwater and, perhaps, the fish were not really fish. Masson, a French army soldier gravely wounded in World War I, often used the canvas to make statements about war. Said Schneede,

> In the sand pictures, Masson tried to break free from the restrictions and rules of painting. What has been gained is a kind of breakthrough, an art that transcends the boundaries of the conventional picture. The thematic content of Battle of the Fish and similar works is the trauma of war translated in the animal world. . . . War and death are important themes in Masson's work; during that period he expressed these themes through his dominant motifs, the bird and the fish.[37]

By the late 1920s Masson found the surrealist movement too confining and started working in far more abstract genres. In the years to come the work of Masson as well as the other surrealists would provide the foundations for many other artists.

The Surrealists' Influences

Surrealism has influenced artists working in other genres, such as the abstract expressionists who dominated the art world in the 1940s and 1950s. Later, the pop art created by Andy Warhol in the 1960s and 1970s employed some of the techniques first explored by the surrealists. Meanwhile, artists working in America and elsewhere, including Dorothea Tanning in the United States and Frida Kahlo in Mexico, explored their own surrealist images and have become recognized as important surrealist artists.

Starting in the late 1930s Dalí, Ernst, and many of the other founding members of the movement fled Europe to escape the clouds of war that hovered over the continent. Many of them settled in America, where they created surrealist art and gave exhibitions of their work but, with the exception of Dalí, preferred to live quietly and out of the spotlight. Still, other artists observed their work and found themselves drawn to the genre and anxious to adapt the techniques of surrealism to their own art. Said Schneede, "Now that Surrealism was beginning to pass into the hands of a new generation, there were new principles, new goals."[38]

Triangular shapes form the figure of the musician in Pablo Picasso's *The Man with a Clarinet.*

Surrealism and Picasso

The surrealists had been influencing other artists long before they crossed the Atlantic Ocean. Among the most renowned of European artists who dabbled in surrealism was Picasso, who had been friendly with Breton and Miró and admired the work of Dalí. Picasso had, of course, been responsible for inspiring Apollinaire to concoct the term for the movement; otherwise, he was very close to Breton and painted the poet's portrait a half-dozen times.

Breton tried to lure Picasso into surrealism. Breton believed that Picasso's 1912 painting *The Man with a Clarinet* was the first truly surrealist painting. The painting, which was rendered in the cubist style, features mostly muted gray and brown tones. The clarinet player is rendered mostly through the use of triangular shapes. Breton suggested that *The Man with a Clarinet* laid the foundation for all future surrealist art:

> *The Man with [a] Clarinet* remains as tangible proof of that which we continue to advance, the knowledge that the spirit obstinately speaks to us of a future continent and that everyone is in a position to accompany an ever-more-beautiful Alice to Wonderland. . . . O Picasso, you have brought to its supreme degree the spirit, not of contradiction, but of evasion: You have allowed to hang from each of your paintings a ladder of cord, even a ladder made with the sheets from your bed, and it is probable that you as well as we are seeking only to come down, to climb up from our sleep.[39]

Still, Picasso never formally joined the surrealist school, preferring to paint, and interpret, what he saw with his own eyes rather than probe the depths of his subconscious for inspiration. But Picasso was fascinated with expressing the dark side of human thought—a fascination he shared with all the surrealists. For example, one of Picasso's paintings, *The Scream*, was used in a 1927 issue of a journal published by Breton to illustrate a poem by surrealist writer Paul Éluard. *The Scream* features an abstract rendering of a woman's face; the surrealist influence can be seen in how Picasso painted the teeth—as though they are daggers.

Surrealism and the Abstract Expressionists

Even though he remained on the periphery of surrealist art, an artist of Picasso's stature nevertheless added authenticity to a movement that was greeted with skepticism outside France. Certainly, Picasso's reputation helped sell surrealism in the United States, where the movement found an audience among young art students who were starting to form their own ideas about abstract expression.

Many American artists had their first exposure to surrealist and dadaist art at a 1936 exhibition at the Museum of Modern Art in New York. Said *Time* magazine, which covered the exhibition,

> Inside the front door of Manhattan's Museum of Modern Art this week, oblong slabs of glass painted with black stripes revolved steadily under a six foot pair of red lips painted by artist Man Ray. In other galleries throughout the building were a black felt hat with a necklace of cinema film and zippers for eyes; a stuffed parrot on a hollow log containing a doll's leg; a teacup, plate and spoon covered entirely with fur; a picture painted entirely on the back of a door which dangled a dollar watch; a plaster crab and a huge board to which were tacked a mousetrap, a pair of baby shoes, a rubber sponge, clothespins, a stiff collar, pearl necklace, a child's umbrella, a braid of auburn hair and a number of hairpins twisted to form a human face.[40]

One of the artists who studied those images was Jackson Pollock, a founder of abstract expressionism. Pollock was fascinated by automatism and sought to use that technique to produce a new school of images.

Abstract expressionists paint wild, bizarre, and colorful scenes that appear to have no logical form. Many do not use normal painting techniques. One of the traits of surrealism that attracted the abstract expressionists was the way the surrealists often commenced their paintings or drawings. In many cases, a surrealist would pick a place on the canvas at random and make a pencil mark or smudge or a streak with a paint brush, and then, through the process of automatism, let the rest of the artwork fall into place. The randomness of surrealist art fascinated the abstract expressionists, and they were eager to commence their paintings in similar fashion.

Pollock studied surrealism and admired the work of Masson, who experimented with a technique in which he would

Jackson Pollock's *She-Wolf* depicts an image of a bull, but curiously, there is no image of a wolf in the painting.

PEGGY GUGGENHEIM

The woman most responsible for introducing surrealism to the American art community was Marguerite Guggenheim, a New York socialite and member of the wealthy Guggenheim family. Born in 1898, Peggy Guggenheim moved to Paris as a young woman where she joined the circle of artists and writers who lived in the French capital following World War I. She became friendly with Marcel Duchamp and Man Ray, for whom she modeled.

She used her inheritance to amass an impressive collection of surrealist art, which included works by Dalí, Miró, Magritte, and Ernst, to whom she was briefly married. During World War II Guggenheim opened an art gallery in New York City that specialized in Dada and surrealism but also featured the works of Jackson Pollock and other American abstract artists. She named the gallery "Art of This Century." In 1942 Time magazine covered its opening and reported,

Gallery goers enter a kind of artistic Coney Island. Here are shadow boxes, peepholes, in one of which, by raising a handle is revealed a brilliantly lighted canvas by Swiss painter Paul Klee. Another peepshow,

manipulated by turning a huge ship's wheel, shows a rotating exhibit of reproductions of all the works, including a miniature toilet for MEN by screwball Surrealist Marcel Duchamp.

Peggy Guggenheim sits beside some of the art she loved.

Quoted in Martica Sawin, *Surrealism in Exile and the Beginning of the New York School.* Cambridge, MA: MIT Press, 1995, p. 233.

simply let the paint from his brush drip onto the canvas. Pollock adopted the drip method and regarded it as a form of automatism. His friend and fellow abstract expressionist, Peter Busa, recalled watching him work. Said Busa, "He talked about the free-agent, the element in Surrealism where you don't touch the canvas, where you let the paint fall."[41]

Still, Pollock and the other American abstract expressionists were not prone to become surrealists themselves. Most of the European surrealists did not speak English. With the exception of Dalí, the surrealists rarely lectured, gave interviews, or accepted students. Wrote May Rosenberg, the wife of influential art critic Harold Rosenberg, "The Surrealists arrived like visiting royalty, bearers of sacred visions to the heathens; trippers among the lollipops."[42]

Pollock looked beyond the insensitivities and the quirkiness of the European surrealists, concentrating mostly on their techniques. As he became an established member of the American abstract art community, Pollock attempted to probe his self-conscious thoughts for inspiration. His 1943 painting *She-Wolf* shows just how much his work was influenced by surrealism. The painting depicts an image of a bull standing against a background of broad streaks of black and curlicues of color. Art critics studied the image hard and were unable to find the image of a wolf in the painting—largely because Pollock had not painted one. Pollock's friend, the artist James Brooks, said that the image clearly formed itself in the deepest part of Pollock's subconscious mind. "[Jackson's] unconscious came through," Brooks said. "In a sense, he walked right into another world."[43]

American Surrealists

Despite the reluctance of the abstract expressionists to fully adopt surrealism, there were some American artists who embraced the genre. When he arrived in America Ernst met Tanning, a New York-based artist. The two would eventually marry. When they met in 1942, Tanning was working on a painting of a seminude woman—a self-portrait—opening a door to reveal a series of other doors opening as well. At her feet crouches a lemur, a tiny monkey found on the island of Madagascar. In this case, though, the monkey is winged. Around the woman's waist Tanning painted a skirt of roots; around the woman's shoulders she painted a puffy-sleeved purple and gold jacket with frilly cuffs, as though the woman has just stepped out of Europe's Renaissance era. Said Schneede,

> If we wanted to assume that the picture has symbolic significance, we might take it for a self-portrait in which the skirt of many roots points to a closeness to nature while the Renaissance jacket may suggest an affinity with art and with the many Renaissance pictures of Venus. In such a context, the open doors could be interpreted as leading to various new beginnings in the artist's life.[44]

Ernst declared that he intended to marry the artist and keep the painting. "I want to spend the rest of my life with Dorothea," he said. "This picture is part of that life."[45]

Another American accepted into the surrealist movement was David Hare, a painter, sculptor, and photographer. Like Man Ray, Hare experimented with the photographer's tools and processes. He found that he could give his negatives an eerie effect by heating them during the development process, which caused the negatives to ripple and distort. He called the process "heatage." Although Hare experimented with surrealist photography, his sculptures are regarded as his most surrealist work. He created complex bronze, steel, and rock sculptures. Hare's sculpture *Sunrise*, which he completed in 1955, features a sunlike figure held aloft over a rocky Earth by metal rods. He also included drops of rain, two moons, and a star. According to Mariann Smith, a curator at the Albright-Knox Art Gallery in Buffalo, New York, where *Sunrise* is on display, *Sunrise* blends the real with the unreal—the basic principle of surrealism. She said,

> There are a number of interesting contrasts in the sculpture. For example, Hare has included elements of both night and day, appropriate for a work of art representing

Dorothea Tanning's self-portrait (pictured) suggests new beginnings, a closeness to nature, and a love of art.

Sunrise. Some of his objects in reality are solid in form, such as the Earth and the moon, while others, such as the sun, star, rain, and clouds are not. There is also a contrast between the smooth, painted steels used to create the clouds, crescent moon, and rain, and the rough bronze that forms the sun, star, and round moon.[46]

Hare would also cement his surrealist credentials by marrying French artist Jacqueline Lamba, who divorced Breton in the 1930s. When Breton arrived in America he collaborated with Hare on the journal *VVV*, which promoted and analyzed surrealist art in the United States.

Surrealism and Pop Art

By the 1960s pop art had become a major force in the American art world. Its most important practitioner was Andy Warhol, whose work includes portraits of Campbell soup cans and oversized replicas of Brillo soap pad boxes. He was also known for colorful portraits of celebrities such as Marilyn Monroe and Elvis Presley. He decorated his New York studio, which he called the "Factory," completely in silver, covering every square inch with silver paint or with Reynolds aluminum foil. This bizarre display of modern art was embraced by art critics who believed Warhol represented the first wave of a new generation of hip artists. To show off the newly decorated studio, Warhol threw a party and invited the press. The reporters and partygoers who saw the Factory decked out in silver must surely have felt the presence of the surrealists in the room with them. Wrote one news reporter, "The whole place is Reynolds wrap, the ceiling, the pipes, the walls. The floor has been painted silver. All the cabinets have been painted silver. The odd assortment of stools and chairs are silver. And the bathroom is silver-lined and painted, including the toilet bowl and flushing mechanism."[47]

Warhol may not have wholeheartedly embraced surrealism, but wrapping an ordinary room floor to ceiling in aluminum foil certainly merged the real world with the unreal. In fact, Warhol had experimented with surrealist techniques for

The *Campbell's Soup Can (Tomato)* became one of pop artist Andy Warhol's most recognizable pieces.

years. During the 1950s he perfected a technique known as the "blotted line." He used pen and ink to draw an image, then blotted a clean sheet of paper over the wet ink to create a runny and abstract form. The blotted line technique helped Warhol define his style; nevertheless, it was a technique closely related to decalcomania, which was perfected by Ernst some thirty years earlier.

And what were Warhol's portraits of Campbell soup cans if not updated versions of Duchamp's Readymades? Experts were hard-pressed to tell the difference between Dada and pop art. Said Bruce H. Hinrichs, a professor of psychology who has studied modern art, "Andy Warhol and other Pop artists painted . . . images of soup cans and similarly mundane, ordinary objects, forcing the viewer to look again and carefully at objects of common perception. The ironic upshot . . . was that

THE DALÍS ARRIVE IN NEW YORK

Salvador Dalí and his wife Gala made a splashy entrance when they arrived in New York. The flamboyant artist was welcomed into New York society by wealthy art lovers who were eager to have him attend their parties, where their guests could gush over the world's most famous surrealist. Reported *Time* magazine, "He was taken up by swank New York socialites and in his honor was held a fancy dress ball that is still the talk of the West Fifties. Madame Dalí wore a dress of transparent red paper and a headdress made of broiled lobsters and a doll's head. Artist Dalí wore a glass case on his chest containing a brassiere."

The Dalís outdid themselves when they visited London a few months later. Scheduled to give a lecture on art, Dalí arrived at the auditorium wearing a deep-sea diving suit and a jeweled dagger stuck in his belt. In one hand he held a billiard cue while in the other the leashes for two large Russian wolfhounds. It was hard to breathe in the suit, though, and Dalí nearly fainted. When the helmet was unscrewed, the surrealist explained, "I just wanted to show that I was plunging deeply into the human mind."

Quoted in "Marvelous and Fantastic," *Time*, December 14, 1936, p. 62.

the Surrealist object was praised for its strangeness and the Pop Art object for its unstrangeness!"[48]

During the 1970s Dalí and his wife Gala made frequent trips to New York. They welcomed Warhol into their circle. Now in his 70s, Dalí had lost none of the flamboyance that catapulted him to fame some forty years before. He carried a gold scepter, gave lavish parties, and enjoyed dining with celebrities in New York's bistros. He always invited the attention of photographers and hoped to see his name in the tabloid newspapers.

By now, Warhol had been making his celebrity portraits by taking photographs of his subjects, then blowing them up into very large prints. Next, he traced the images on canvas, then used the blotted line technique to give them an abstract feel. Finally, Warhol colored them—often with incandescent tones. Although the portraits are not regarded as surrealist work, Warhol's technique did give the images a surrealist look. Dalí admired them greatly, but when Warhol offered to photograph Gala Dalí for one of the portraits, the artist flatly refused. "The strength of Gala is in her privacy," he insisted. "Gala never is photographed!"[49] To make Warhol feel better, though, Dalí did acknowledge to the pop artist that he had risen to second place on the list of Dalí's favorite artists. First place was, of course, still held by Dalí himself.

There is no question that Warhol was influenced by the techniques of surrealism, but he was never one to probe the depths of his subconscious thought—he was much more at home gossiping with celebrities at New York City discos. But he was the type of artist who delighted in shocking the public, and for that he owed a great debt to the surrealists.

The Movement in Mexico

The surrealists' influence was not confined to American artists such as Pollock, Tanning, and Warhol; surrealists were also influencing artists such as Kahlo in Mexico. Kahlo had suffered through many personal tragedies. Her right leg was deformed by polio. As a young girl she witnessed the bloodshed of the

Mexican Revolution. As a medical student she was severely injured in a bus accident that would force her to drop out of medical school and live in pain for the rest of her life. The accident also damaged her reproductive organs, making it impossible for her to have children.

She used art to reveal her psychological distress. Kahlo produced 143 paintings in her lifetime, about a third of which were self-portraits. Her 1946 self-portrait *The Little Deer* is a typical example of Kahlo's surrealism. The painting depicts Kahlo's head on the body of a deer which has been pierced by arrows. Art historian Hayden Herrera said the painting tells a lot about Kahlo's tortured life:

> In *The Little Deer* Frida presents herself with the body of a young stag and her own head crowned with antlers. Like Frida, the deer is prey to suffering. Pierced by nine arrows, he stares out at the viewer from a forest enclosure. . . .
>
> The deer's youthful vigor contrasts with the decay of old tree trunks, whose broken branches and knots correspond to his wounds. Beneath him a slender branch broken from a young tree alludes to Frida's and the deer's broken youth and imminent death. . . .
>
> In Aztec belief the deer was the sign for the right foot; even with Frida's various operations, the condition of her right foot continued to worsen, and the deer could have been a kind of talisman. The arrows in the deer may, like the arrows in valentine hearts, point to pain in love.[50]

Kahlo met Breton in 1938 during a visit by the surrealist poet to Mexico. He was impressed with her work and used his contacts to arrange for an exhibition of her art in New York. Kahlo was one of several Mexican artists who experimented with surrealism. Others included Kahlo's husband, Diego Rivera, who also painted in the cubist style; José Clemente Orozco, whose large murals often featured surrealist images (although the international surrealist community found him personally repugnant because of his support for fascism and, in particular, Adolph Hitler); and David Alfaro Siqueiros, who used colors as brightly and boldly as Dalí.

Another Mexican surrealist was Leonora Carrington. British-born, she met Ernst in France and worked closely with him. When the Germans invaded France, Carrington fled to Spain, where she suffered a mental breakdown. She was hospitalized in Portugal, where she was given powerful antipsychotic drugs. Picasso learned of her plight and arranged for her to accompany a diplomat to Mexico, where she married and took citizenship. In Mexico she painted in the surrealist style. Typical of her surrealist work is the 1945 painting *The Pleasures of Dagobert*, which features dozens of surreal images—fire, volcanoes, forests, a winding staircase, a woman adrift in a

Leonora Carrington was born in Great Britain but her talent for surrealism blossomed in Mexico.

small boat, a beast rising from a pool of water, a ghostly apparition streaking overhead, and a bearded king led on horseback by a child, among others. According to British art historian Dawn Ades, Carrington's talent for surrealism blossomed in Mexico, where she found a country entering modern civilization while slowly shaking off the mystical beliefs and practices of its people. Carrington enjoyed wading into the street markets of old Mexican cities, where she listened to the tall tales told by the vendors. Carrington was fascinated by the "magic" potions sold by street vendors, and she also believed in alchemy. Clearly, Ades said, Carrington drew inspiration for *The Pleasures of Dagobert* from her forays into Mexican mysticism:

> Carrington portrays here, with the luminous clarity of her egg tempera technique, complete imaginary worlds. . . . The different landscapes correspond to the four elements of alchemy and medieval natural history: earth, air, fire and water. There is a definite rhythm to their placings: the dry, ghastly extinct volcanoes of the Valley of Mexico are juxtaposed on one side with a lake of fire engulfing an inverted idol, and on the other with a watery world where a hairy giant with a double animal head holds out a human-faced puffer fish. Transformations, of the elements, of human, animal, plant, of animate and inanimate, occur at every point.[51]

Carrington said that many of these images came to her while she fought through the quagmire of mental illness. She said, "I was . . . the Moon, the Holy Ghost, a gypsy, an acrobat, Leonora Carrington and a woman."[52] But it was Kahlo who Breton declared had most sincerely captured the passion of surrealism in Mexico. He wrote, "The art of Frida Kahlo is a ribbon around a bomb."[53]

Surrealism and Social Change

Breton and the other early surrealists were drawn to left-wing politics and supported the socialists, Communists, and anarchists who attempted to gain a foothold in post–World War I Europe. The surrealists believed the war was caused by a small number of wealthy industrialists and others who sought to profit from the bloodshed of others. Breton and the other surrealists believed that the common people—the workers—should rise up against the power of the industrialists. He said,

> If this were religion, the fervor of our intentions alone would have been enough. The Surrealists in particular gave much of themselves. They had adhered to the view that what was still—and by far—most shocking about the world around them was the subservience in which a miniscule part of the human race held the rest, without any justification whatsoever. Of all the evils, this was the most intolerable, since it was entirely within man's power to remedy.[54]

While many of the surrealist artists followed Breton into socialism, unlike Breton few of them sought to become influential in the international socialist movement. Instead, most of the surrealists preferred using their art to make political statements. As the surrealists fled Europe during World War II, many would use their paintings to denounce war. Following the war surrealism continued to carry a political message, often in support of public uprisings against corrupt or repressive regimes. For decades, many political movements have looked toward surrealism for inspiration.

More than an Intellectual

Breton was more than just an intellectual socialist. He wrote about socialism, addressed assemblies, and traveled extensively, actively promoting the socialist cause. In 1938 he visited exiled Soviet Communist leader Leon Trotsky in Mexico, where he had been befriended by Kahlo and Rivera. Trotsky, Breton, and Rivera drew up a manifesto, *Towards a Revolutionary Art*, that called for artists and writers to use their skills in support of socialism. Said the manifesto, "The communist revolution is not afraid of art. It realizes that the role of the artist in a decadent capitalist society is determined by the conflict between the individual and various social forms which are hostile to him. This fact alone, insofar as he is conscious of it, makes the artist the natural ally of revolution."[55]

Later, in a socialist magazine that Breton edited, which was titled *Clé* (in English, *Key*), he wrote that art should be the universal voice of the socialist movement. "Art has no country, just as the workers have none,"[56] Breton insisted.

Many of the surrealist artists were not as active politically as Breton; instead, they chose to speak through their canvases. Most of the early surrealist artists dabbled in the ideology espoused by the German writer Karl Marx, whose 1848 book *The Communist Manifesto* inspired the leaders of the Bolshevik revolution in Russia and led to the establishment of the Soviet Union. The surrealists were interested in what Marx had to say and not just because they felt workers had been abused by factory owners. Marx also advocated a breakdown of many of the principles of cultured society—he advocated the abolition of marriage and the recognition of free love as an acceptable

lifestyle. (Men and women should be free to sleep with whomever they desired.) The early surrealists, swapping partners and leading bohemian lifestyles on Paris's Left Bank, probably could not have agreed more.

Marx's political goals—establishment of a workers' utopia—struck a chord with the surrealists. Man Ray's credentials as a socialist dated back to his early days in New York before he left for Paris to join the surrealist movement. He was acquainted with socialist agitator Emma Goldman and designed two covers for her magazine *Mother Earth*.

Artists André Breton (far left), Diego Rivera (second from left), and Jacqueline Lamba (far right) meet with Communist leader Leon Trotsky in Mexico.

George Grosz used his art to agitate against authority. Born in 1893 in Berlin, he joined the German army in 1914 out of a sense of patriotism but soon became disillusioned with the cause and was discharged from the military after being deemed unfit to serve. Once out of the army, Grosz joined the German Communist party.

He soon soured on communism as well. Following the armistice, Grosz spent six months in Russia, where he met Bolshevik leaders Vladimir Lenin and Leon Trotsky. Grosz found their rule too dictatorial for his liking and returned to Germany, where he found a chaotic postwar democracy. He used his art to lampoon the incompetent leaders of the Weimar Republic. A typical painting from this era is *Fit for Active Service*, which he painted in 1919. Said art historians H.H. Arnason, Marla F. Prather, and Daniel Wheeler, "This work shows Grosz's sense of the macabre and his detestation of bureaucracy, with a fat complacent doctor pronouncing his 'OK' of a desiccated cadaver before arrogant Prussian-type officers."

Grosz fled Germany in 1932 after the Nazis came to power. He settled in America and took U.S. citizenship, using his art to denounce the Nazis. He returned to Berlin in 1959. Grosz died that year after falling down a stairwell.

Fit for Active Service *(shown) shows George Grosz's sense of the macabre.*

Quoted in H.H. Arnason, Marla F. Prather, and Daniel Wheeler, *History of Modern Art.* New York: Harry N. Abrams, 1998, p. 285.

One of the most prominent artists of the era to espouse Communist sympathies was George Grosz, who is regarded as a dadaist but whose work often contains strong surrealist images. His most famous painting, *Republican Automatons*, which he painted in 1920, shows two gentlemen standing on a Berlin street. One of the fellows has no face; instead, the number 12 is printed across his blank head. The other man in the picture has no top to his head; words and numerals pour out of the opening. Grosz envisioned his fellow Germans as robots following the dictates of the incompetent Weimar government without question. In the painting one of the robots holds aloft the German flag. Grosz is given credit for steering Dada toward promoting political messages—a trend that would be embraced by the surrealists. Said art historians H.H. Arnason, Marla F. Prather, and Daniel Wheeler, "Empty-headed, blank-faced, and mutilated automatons parade loyally through the streets of a mechanistic metropolis on their way to vote as they are told. In such words as this, Grosz comes closest to the spirit of the Dadaists and Surrealists."[57]

The Spanish Civil War

Like Grosz, many surrealists found inspiration in World War I and its aftermath. Another conflict would soon brew on the European continent, touching the lives of some surrealists and influencing their work and their private lives. The Spanish Civil War lasted from 1936 until 1939 and resulted in a victory for the fascists under General Francisco Franco, who would go on to lead Spain until his death in 1975. Among the opponents who fought against Franco were socialists. The dictator treated his opponents harshly, lining up captured prisoners in front of firing squads in his campaign to wipe out socialism in Spain.

Many of the surrealists sided with the socialists. Masson's 1937 painting *Hora de Todos* (in English, *Hour of All*) is rendered in grays and blacks and displays many tortured faces. Masson intended the painting as a statement against the bloodshed of the Spanish conflict. Magritte contributed *Le*

Drapeau Noir (in English, *The Black Flag*), which shows bizarre flying machines hovering in a dark sky over a barren landscape. During the civil war Franco enlisted the German army to bomb enemy positions in the town of Guernica. As many as sixteen hundred Spaniards are believed to have lost their lives in the bombing. Magritte produced the painting in response to the massacre. "The first, and also the last, impression the painting makes on us is one of a threat hanging over the world," said Hammacher. "The color is somber, hard, and menacing, and the draftsmanship of the construction is as simple as it is relentlessly accurate."[58]

Dalí also made his own statements against war. In 1934 Dalí and his wife Gala left Paris for a lecture in the Spanish city of Barcelona. It was there that Dalí first sensed the country was heading toward revolution. Barcelona was in turmoil: Workers were on strike, while a group of anarchists demonstrated in the streets. Dalí was unable to give the lecture—conditions were not deemed safe. The Dalís returned to Paris. Shaken by the experience, Dalí showed his fear for the future of his country in his paintings. In 1936 he produced *Soft Construction with Boiled Beans—Premonition of Civil War*. The image shows a tortured figure standing over a desolate landscape. Grappling and clawing beneath the figure are twisted, emaciated arms and legs. Meanwhile, all that is left of value in the countryside is a handful of scattered beans. The painting represents Dalí's vision for the future of Spain after the war. He said,

> I painted a geological landscape that had been uselessly revolutionized for thousands of years congealed in its "normal course." The soft structure of that great mass of flesh in civil war I embellished with a few boiled beans, for one could not imagine swallowing all that unconscious meat without the presence (however uninspiring) of some mealy and melancholy vegetable.[59]

According to Robert Goff, the painting required little interpretation:

With the gnarled head and hands of the figure at the center of *Soft Construction with Boiled Beans*, Dalí makes the point that the impending Spanish Civil War will be a calamity of tragic, cannibalistic destruction. The parched landscape and tumultuous sky are ominous signs of deprivation and disaster. Boiled beans depict poverty and wartime scarcity.[60]

Dalí's feelings about the coming war were undoubtedly influenced by the poet Federico García Lorca, who had been instrumental in fomenting antifascism among many Spaniards.

Hora de Todos, by André Masson, is a statement against the bloodshed of the Spanish Civil War.

Dalí met García Lorca in 1923, when both men resided in a students' residence hall in Madrid. As a student in Madrid, Dalí espoused anarchy and radical politics, although these positions would soften in later years. García Lorca did not soften his antifascist positions; eventually, he would be murdered by agents acting under Franco's orders.

Miró, also a Spaniard, opposed Franco as well. In 1937 he produced a poster for Franco's opponents that was employed by the movement's leaders to rally opposition to the fascists. The poster shows an opponent of fascism with a raised fist and the caption, "In the current struggle I see the antiquated forces of Fascism on one side, and, on the other those of the people, whose immense creative resources will give Spain a drive that will amaze the world."[61]

Rising from the Ashes

Miró and Dalí remained in France during the Spanish Civil War. As fascism grew in Germany, the surrealists used their paintings to warn of the coming Nazi threat. Dalí's 1939 painting *Beach Scene with Telephone* shows the gigantic handset of a telephone perched in front of a lake. According to Dalí, the telephone represents the fruitless conversations between British prime minister Neville Chamberlain and Adolph Hitler that resulted in the Munich Pact, which delivered Czechoslovakia to Nazi hands and set the stage for World War II. To punctuate this point, Dalí drew two snails crawling over the telephone—symbols that peace negotiations were moving too slowly. Another significant image in the painting is the skeleton of a wooden sailing ship. "There is a pervading sense of melancholy and decay," said Moorehouse. "The receiver hangs from a crutch, its cord draped limply from a second, similar support, suggesting that the lines of communication are dead. Snails crawl over the telephone, symbolizing the protracted and hopeless nature of the negotiations. On the horizon the wreck of a boat, the spars of its hull exposed like a ribcage, evokes the end of a voyage."[62]

Of course, the devastation of World War II would not touch Dalí personally. He waited out the war years in the

A Miró poster urges opposition to Spain's fascist government and support for Spaniards trying to defeat the government.

United States in comfort, enjoying the attention of his wealthy American admirers. Dalí fully embraced his new home and thoroughly loved the American people as well as their democracy. His 1943 painting *Geopoliticus Child Watching the Birth of the New Man* depicts Earth in the shape of an egg. Tearing away the eggshell is an adult man who emerges from the North American continent. Europe, on the other hand, is portrayed by the artist as a very minor land mass. Dalí's message was clear: The Americans would rise from the ashes of World War II as the leaders of a new world order.

Dalí's countryman, Miró, also lived in France during the Spanish Civil War and, like Dalí, was forced to flee France as war in Europe grew near. He could not return to Spain, where Franco would have had him arrested. Instead, he hid on the island of Majorca off the coast of Spain until he could safely return to France after World War II.

Ripped Apart by War

As the Nazis gained power and swept through Europe, they wrathfully targeted the surrealist artists. Hitler—a failed artist himself—abhorred abstract art and directed the Nazi party to conduct public burnings of abstract works. Masson found himself the target of Nazi wrath. He escaped and made his way to the United States, where his artwork was seized at the U.S. Customs station by agents who regarded it as pornographic. Incredibly, the customs agents ripped up Masson's paintings as the artist looked on in horror.

Masson spent the war in Connecticut. Undaunted by his cold reception, Masson continued to paint and used his art to denounce the Nazi regime. His 1942 painting *There Is No Finished World* was intended as an antiwar statement. It depicts a fight between two abstract figures while a third figure, a minotaur—a man with a bull's head—watches from the side. In Masson's mind, the minotaur represented death.

At least Masson managed to escape the Nazis. Ernst was not so lucky. Arrested in 1939, Ernst spent two years in Les Milles, a labor camp where he was put to work making bricks.

In the camp he met Bellmer, also a surrealist. While in detention, Bellmer painted a portrait of Ernst—it depicts the sullen artist, his face composed of bricks against a stark black background.

Ernst was released in 1941 (he was helped across the French border by an art-loving guard) and made his way to America, where he used his art to depict Europe in the throes of warfare. Among these paintings is *Europe After the Rain II* from 1942, which shows a soldier with the head of a bird wading through a field of ruins and desolation. For the painting Ernst used the decalcomania technique, which helped enhance the feeling he had tried to convey of a decaying countryside. Said Faerna, "This method proved ideal for Ernst's prefiguration of the desolation and death that would descend over Europe at the conclusion of the war."[63] Another Ernst painting, *The Temptations of St. Anthony*, which the artist painted in 1945, shows hideous beasts tearing at the flesh of St. Anthony. The background of this chaotic scene is dominated by a serene European landscape. Clearly, Ernst intended the beasts to represent the Nazis while St. Anthony represented the pious and devoted citizens of Europe who were ripped apart by the war.

Ernst spent the early years of the war in New York. In 1943 Ernst and Tanning, now his wife, settled in Sedona, Arizona. Ernst was completely taken with his new home and enjoyed the "cowboy" lifestyle. His neighbors often saw the German surrealist clad in blue jeans as he hiked among the mesas and canyons of the Sedona landscape. Ernst lived in Sedona until 1953, when he returned to Paris. He told his friends that there were only two places in the world where he would want to live; one was Paris, the other Sedona.

As for Dalí, he returned to Spain in 1949 where he was welcomed home as a hero by Franco. Dalí's longing to return to Spain was evidently a much greater force in his life than the memory of his friend, García Lorca, who had been murdered on Franco's orders. Indeed, Dalí congratulated the dictator for bringing order to the country and wiping out the subversive elements. "I have reached the conclusion," he said, "that (Franco)

LES MILLES

The labor camp where Max Ernst was imprisoned for two years at the outset of World War II was known as Les Milles because it was located near a French town of that name. At first, the camp was used to hold Germans who were living in France at the time of the Nazi invasion of that country. Later, the Nazis used Les Milles as a concentration camp, where French Jews and other victims of the Third Reich were held before their deportation to Auschwitz and other death camps.

Ironically, when he was arrested by the French police, Ernst was working on a surrealist landscape titled *A Moment of Calm*. The painting depicts a colorful landscape under a serene sky.

Les Milles included a brick factory, where Ernst was put to work. His cellmate was Hans Bellmer, another German surrealist artist. Although Ernst won his release from custody, Bellmer remained imprisoned for the duration of the war. Bellmer survived the war, returned to Paris, and went on to create surrealist drawings and photographs.

is a saint."[64] Dalí's embrace of the fascist dictator further infuriated Breton and the other leaders of the surrealist movement. Dalí brushed off their criticisms. He had always regarded himself as the only true surrealist and, therefore, did not need the friendship or support of the others. He lived the rest of his life near his boyhood home in the Catalonia region of Spain, although he often traveled and enjoyed the busy nightlife of New York and other big cities. He painted when the mood inspired him, although his output did decline as he grew older. His work also became far less political; still, he had no regrets. In 1953 Dalí summed up his life. "Every morning upon awakening," he said, "I experience a supreme pleasure: that of being Salvador Dalí, and I ask myself, wonderstruck, what prodigious thing will he do today, this Salvador Dalí."[65]

The Situationists

While Dalí relaxed in Catalonia and stayed out of Spanish politics, across the Mediterranean Sea in the Italian village of Cosio di Arroscia, a small group of intellectuals, political agitators, and artists met in 1957 to form a new group, which they named Situationist International. They espoused Marxism, but their philosophy was based on much more than just socialist ideology. They believed that politicians and industrialists had caused wars, forced people to live in poverty, and allowed crime to take over the streets. They also believed that the ideas of truly creative people had been stifled. They decided that art—and in particular, surrealist art—should be the guiding force in society. To promote social change, they advocated labor strikes, riots, and other sudden "situations." The society that would emerge would be surreal—the realness of everyday life suddenly disrupted by an unreal event, as though the whole world was the canvas of a sprawling surrealist painting.

Situationism—as the movement was called—never really caught on. What is more, over the years the situationists fought among themselves and divided into various splinter groups. But they remained heavily influenced by surrealism: Their leader, Guy Debord, was a devoted student of Breton's writings. One of the founding members of Situationist International was the English surrealist artist Ralph Rumney, who was the son-in-law of Peggy Guggenheim, a wealthy American art collector and benefactor who in the 1930s helped introduce surrealist art in the United States. Rumney believed that cities could be redesigned through automatism—that planners could wander through a city designing streets, bridges, buildings, fountains, sidewalks, and other urban features wherever their imaginations took them. Rumney applied his theory to a redesign for Venice, Italy, and proposed that the city's famous canals be dyed bright green. "Situationism," Rumney said, "was artistic, political and philosophical games, which provoked an extreme reaction, and which put you back in touch with real experience, real life."[66]

Rumney's 1957 surrealist painting *The Change* hangs in London's famed Tate Gallery. The colorful abstract work shows stabs of paint over a grid of black streaks. According to the Tate's catalog, "The combination of chance marks and the ordering device of a grid has been interpreted as a visual metaphor for the interaction of the subconscious and conscious, as well as the spiritual and material."[67]

Rumney was welcomed into surrealist circles after marrying Peggy Guggenheim's daughter, Pegeen. When Pegeen took her own life in 1967 in the couple's Paris home, her mother accused Rumney of abetting the suicide. Rumney's former mother-in-law had him trailed by detectives, which eventually forced him to flee to London, where he arrived penniless. He took a job as a telephone operator and painted only sporadically, dying of cancer in 2002.

Even the situationists, the movement he helped found, abandoned him. In 1958, just a few months after the movement was established in Italy, Rumney received a letter from Debord kicking him out because he missed a deadline for submitting an article to the movement's journal. Said the letter, "Of course we like you a lot, but you can understand that we don't make a habit of endlessly prolonging negligence in certain affairs, in which you, like us, have chosen to be involved."[68]

Paris, 1968

As bizarre as their ideas may have seemed, the situationists nearly had a chance to test their theories. In 1968 widespread student rioting and labor strikes broke out in Paris. Leftist students occupied La Sorbonne. During the uprising the walls of the university were covered with such situationist-inspired slogans as "Abolish Class Society," "Terminate the University," and "Occupy the Factories."[69] For days anarchy ruled the streets of Paris. For a brief period it appeared as though the French government would fall, providing the situationists with the surreal society they had long sought.

French authorities soon contained the uprising and returned calm to the city. To pacify the labor unions French industrialists agreed to pay higher wages to the workers. As for the students, without the backing of the labor unions their dreams of forcing a socialist takeover of the government were thwarted. Still painting in 1968, Miró honored the situationist cause by producing the surrealist painting *May 1968*, which shows splashes and drips of black paint, colorful splotches,

Labor strikers march through Paris in 1968.

stark black lines, and handprints—all depicting the chaos and ultimate downfall of the movement. "The picture seems like an obituary of the student revolts in Paris in May 1968. Miró always saw himself as a 'man of revolt,' revolting against apathy and hypocrisy," said German art historian Walter Erben. "Miró's universe is untouchable. His revolution has taken place on the playing field of the canvas. However, it continues to make itself felt in our minds."[70]

Surrealism Today

The original surrealists have left behind a rich legacy of paintings, photographs, sculptures, and other works that have earned their places among the greatest art created in the twentieth century. Major American art museums regularly schedule exhibits of surrealist paintings. Typically, thousands of people attend the exhibitions. During an exhibition, it is not unusual for visitors to spend several minutes in front of a painting by Dalí trying to figure out exactly what the artist was thinking—or more appropriately, dreaming—when he envisioned the image.

Once those visitors leave the museums, they may not find the work by Dalí and the other surrealists that much different from what they see in the movies or on TV or in the pages of a magazine. Indeed, today's popular culture is filled with surrealist images. TV commercials, movies, music videos, photography—and yes, even paintings—are regularly produced with the surrealist's eye for the bizarre.

Blue Lips in Space

TV commercials have, in fact, become a place where surrealist directors can display their talents. For example, when the Nissan

Like other surrealist art, *Lost Highway* tried to interpret the filmmaker's dreams. Pictured is a scene from the movie.

car company planned an advertising campaign for a new model, the Micra, it turned to American film director David Lynch to develop a TV commercial that would make the vehicle appeal to young drivers with a taste for the offbeat. Lynch responded by producing a commercial showing the Micra cruising down a rain-splashed city street in Paris. In the ad the sky is blue-black, but the buildings that line the street are brightly lit. In one of the buildings a woman with red hair watches as the car cruises by. Finally, overhead, a gigantic pair of blue lips that hover in space speak a few, indecipherable words. In fact, the words themselves spill forth in text from the lips as they are spoken.

Nissan's TV commercial oozes surrealism, from the blue-black sky to the red hair of the woman to the blue lips suspended in space. After all, Man Ray suspended red lips over a French landscape in his 1934 painting *Observatory Time—The Lovers*, and many surrealist artists have added words in text to their paintings, including Grosz's 1920 painting *Republican Automatons*, which shows indecipherable words spilling forth from the empty head of his robot.

Appropriate Home for Surrealism

The cinema has always served as an appropriate home for surrealism. When Nissan decided it needed the touch of a surrealist for its Micra commercial, it chose the right director in Lynch. Many of his movies have included surrealist images. Among his films is the creepy 1986 thriller *Blue Velvet*, which opens with a close-up of a severed human ear; a few minutes later, the camera focuses on slimy beetles grappling with one another beneath the calmness of a manicured lawn. He also directed the 1997 film *Lost Highway*, a bizarre story of a wife killer who finds himself morphing into other characters. The film includes the sudden appearance of a house burning in a desert, and in one chilling surreal sequence the killer encounters a man who calls him on the phone—even though the man is standing in front of him, and grinning, during the conversation. Film critic Jack Matthews said *Lost Highway* followed a key rule of surrealism: It attempted to interpret the filmmaker's dreams. "It is a fascinating, dream-like psychological mind game, with Lynch finding beetles not beneath the surface of polite society but inside the individual human psyche," Matthews said. "*Lost Highway* is less a psychological thriller than a psychoanalytic mystery, and even if you know the meaning of dreams, it will keep you guessing."[71]

Lynch, along with other film directors such as Terry Gilliam, David Cronenberg, and Spike Jonze—whose real name is Adam Spiegel—are regarded as the top surrealist directors working in American cinema today. Although Lynch has concentrated on dark mysteries and Cronenberg is best known for his horror stories, surrealist cinema can also be light and funny. Gilliam has made a number of comedies—his 1998 film *Fear and Loathing in Las Vegas* features a scene in a casino bar populated by lizards sipping cocktails—while Jonze directed one of the weirdest films of the past decade, *Being John Malkovich.* The film, written by Charlie Kaufman and starring John Cusack, tells the story of a puppeteer who finds a hidden door that allows him to enter the brain of the film and theater actor John Malkovich. In the film's most surreal scene, Malkovich discovers the door and enters his own brain. Looking out through his own eyes, Malkovich sees a surreal Malkovichian world: Everyone—men, women, children—has his head, the only words anyone speaks are "Malkovich," and the only words printed in books, newspapers, restaurant menus, and so on are "Malkovich." Summing up the work of cinema's modern surrealists, *Times of London* film critic Ian Johns wrote,

> Lynch, like Terry Gilliam and David Cronenberg, is a rare breed of filmmaker with Surrealist tendencies. His brand of suburban surreal in *Blue Velvet* spawned a thousand crazed TV neighborhoods. . . . And Charlie Kaufman, author of *Being John Malkovich,* in which puppeteer John Cusack finds a portal into the actor's brain, is developing a casual Surrealism that delights a mainstream audience bored by effects-laden extravaganzas that can turn any object into surreal life.[72]

Dalí and Buñuel

Surrealist filmmaking dates back at least to 1928, when Dalí and the Spanish-born director Luis Buñuel collaborated on a number of short films. One of the films they made together,

Un Chien Andalou (in English, *An Andalusian Dog*), includes several squeamish scenes of bloodletting, including the depiction of an eyeball being sliced with a razor blade. Two years later Dalí and Buñuel collaborated again on a full-length film, *L'Âge d'Or* (in English, *The Golden Age*), which opens with a brief documentary about scorpions—and how their stings could be deadly—and then morphs into a story about two lovers whose passion for each other is constantly interrupted. The film includes scenes that Catholic leaders in France regarded as blasphemous. As a result, many theater owners refused to show the film. Cinema owners brave enough to screen the film often saw their theaters vandalized by rioters.

Giant lizards sip cocktails in one of many surreal scenes in *Fear and Loathing in Las Vegas*.

TERRY GILLIAM

*A*merican film director Terry Gilliam brings a touch of surrealism to nearly all his projects. Among his films are *The Fisher King*, a study of two troubled individuals that features the image of a flaming horse galloping across New York's Central Park, and *Brazil*, a futurist look at an oppressed society that includes scenes of a winged man as well as a large stony hand emerging from the earth.

Gilliam has been creating surrealism on film for decades. In the 1960s and 1970s he provided the bizarre and surrealist animations for the hit British comedy series, *Monty Python's Flying Circus*. "We'd never seen anything like these brilliant cartoons before," said *Python* star Michael Palin. "Wonderful pictures, like a church with spires coming off and rockets shooting out."

Born in 1940, Gilliam grew up in Los Angeles. Among his inspirations are the TV shows produced in the 1950s by comedian Ernie Kovacs, who staged a number of surreal sketches, including a production of the ballet *Swan Lake* performed by dancers in gorilla suits, men playing poker in time to Beethoven's *Fifth Symphony*, and an empty office, in which the pencils, clocks, water coolers, pencil sharpeners, and other implements seem to come to life while keeping pace with the background music.

Terry Gilliam has created many surrealist films.

Quoted in Richard Corliss and James Inverne, "Terry's Flying Circus," *Time*, August 8, 2005, p. 64.

During the filming Dalí and Buñuel had a falling out. The controversy over *L'Âge d'Or* finished—at least temporarily—both of their careers in French cinema, although Dalí continued to dabble in filmmaking from time to time. In 1945 he designed the dream sequence that British director Alfred Hitchcock filmed for his murder mystery *Spellbound*. A year later Dalí collaborated with American animation mogul Walt Disney on the production of a six-minute cartoon titled *Destino*. Set to Spanish music, the cartoon has no plot. It simply follows a young ballerina as she travels through a dreamy landscape dominated by creatures and images one would expect to see in a Dalí painting. The cartoon was not released until 2004—long after the deaths of Disney and Dalí—when Disney's heirs resurrected the long-forgotten surrealist cartoon and issued it in a DVD version.

Meanwhile, the torch for French cinematic surrealism was carried by Jean Cocteau, who also directed theater and ballet. In addition to *Beauty and the Beast,* Cocteau directed *Orphée* in 1948, which was an updated version of the Greek mythological story *Orpheus*. The film followed Orphée's attempt to rescue his wife from the underworld. Cocteau included many surrealist images: His characters walked through mirrors; messengers from the underworld were dressed as leather-clad motorcyclists, and the underworld itself was depicted as the bombed-out buildings of France left behind by World War II. By including such diverse images— some taken from real life, some make-believe—Cocteau fulfilled the surrealist's challenge of combining the real with the unreal. Bettina L. Knapp, an art historian and Cocteau's biographer, said *Orphée* is a prime example of surrealism on film: "One might infer then that art can thrive . . . from anything in daily life whether it be animal, mineral, or vegetable: a theory enunciated by the . . . Dadaists, and Surrealists long ago. Cocteau still believed in this axiom, that any animate or inanimate object within creative man's experience can be transformed into a thing of beauty in eternally appealing form."[73]

Actors play their roles in a scene from *Orphée,* an example of French cinematic surrealism.

As for Buñuel, after his dispute with Dalí he left France and emigrated to Mexico, where he made mainstream movies and took citizenship. Following World War II, Buñuel's interest in surrealist cinema reemerged. In 1950 he directed the Mexican film *Los Olvidados* (in English, *The Forgotten Ones*). The film tells the story of impoverished youths struggling to survive in Mexico; its surrealist images include a scene of a cracked egg oozing its contents as well as a dream sequence shot in slow motion. He returned to French cinema in 1972 when he directed his greatest triumph, *Le Charme Discret de la*

Bourgeoisie (in English, *The Discreet Charm of the Bourgeoisie*), which won the Academy Award for best foreign film. "Bourgeoisie" is a French term for the middle class; Karl Marx—whose philosophy has inspired generations of surrealists—regarded the bourgeoisie as an enemy of the working class. Certainly, Buñuel did not intend for the film to shed a positive light on middle-class life.

Buñuel's film contains a confusing series of surreal scenes: diners meeting at a restaurant where a funeral is taking place, soldiers arriving at the restaurant for dinner, theatergoers watching the action of the movie unfold on a stage, and various dream sequences, among others. The characters accept all these features and events as though they are natural, everyday occurrences. Said Ian Johns, "Far from causing riots, Buñuel's *The Discreet Charm of the Bourgeoisie* won the best Foreign Language Film Oscar in 1972. It's a far cry from the days when he and Dalí stuck a razor in cinema's eye with *Un Chien Andalou.* But its legacy can still be felt—albeit nowadays probably in a car commercial."[74]

Tribute to Buñuel

There is no question that car commercials—and other commercials as well—may be one outlet for surrealist directors. Another important platform for contemporary surrealism is music video. Indeed, if surrealism has found a home in TV advertising and in the cinema, it has flourished on MTV and the other television networks that feature music videos.

Anybody who tunes to MTV or similar networks is likely to see singers and dancers performing against backdrops of barren deserts, tropical seascapes, bizarre alien planets, and in front of abstract backgrounds designed to appeal to the weird and funky tastes of the viewers. In many cases the little dramas played out in the videos appear to have nothing to do with the stories told in the lyrics of the songs.

Jonze has directed dozens of music videos. Among the performers who have been featured in his videos are such diverse singers as hip-hop stars Ludacris, Fatboy Slim, and Notorious

B.I.G.; Sean Lennon, the son of the late Beatle John Lennon; and the alternative rock star Björk. Jonze directed the video for Björk's 1995 song *It's Oh So Quiet.* The video shows the singer from Iceland strolling down the center of a small American town, where she is joined in dance by a number of elderly women, a walking mailbox, and several Roman-style columns.

When *Boston Globe* music writer Wesley Morris saw the 2004 video that Jonze directed for the punk-rock group Yeah Yeah Yeahs, he was immediately reminded of the film *Un Chien Andalou.* In the video for the song *Y Control*, a group of ten-year-olds go berserk and attack lead singer Karen O. Wrote Morris, "Singer Karen O and her band appear to be performing at the most exuberantly sick 10-year-old birthday party ever. It's in part a tribute to Buñuel's 1929 silent *Un Chien Andalou.* The setting is a dank parking garage, and Jonze's lighting is cheap horror-movie stuff that catches a dozen or so kids wilding out. They bite Karen O's neck, bust through the walls, axe off a hand, rip out intestines, and do a ritual dance around a dead dog. One kid scribbles on the wall, 'We are going to hell.' Dude, it looks like you're already there."[75]

Surrealism on the Computer

Despite surrealism's influence on movies, TV commercials, and music videos, the genre has always been an art form most at home hanging on the wall of a gallery. Although the great artists of surrealism have now been dead for decades, the genre has been kept alive by many contemporary painters and photographers.

One of the top surrealists working today is fashion photographer David LaChapelle. In 2006 *American Photo* magazine featured a retrospective of his work and included several of his most familiar images on its pages. Among them were his 1998 image *Madonna in Bombay in New York*, which features the pop singer Madonna curled up in a giant purple hand, which is itself set up in a dingy public lavatory; and *Elton John at Home*, shot in 1997 and featuring singer Elton John standing

Born in 1969, surrealist photographer David LaChapelle became hooked on photography after taking his first picture—an image of his mother on the beach. After studying photography at the North Carolina School for the Arts, LaChapelle moved to New York where his talent was recognized by pop art leader Andy Warhol. He worked closely with Warhol, who assigned LaChapelle to take photographs for the celebrity gossip magazine he published, *Interview*.

LaChapelle has branched out into documentary and music video directing. He has directed videos featuring Britney Spears, Elton John, Christina Aguilera, Mariah Carey, Macy Gray, Avril Lavigne, and Jennifer Lopez.

As for photography, he was one of the first major commercial photographers to embrace digital imaging, using the computer to enhance the surreal aspects of his images. He cautions young photographers to be wary of the process, suggesting that no amount of manipulation on the computer can improve a poor photograph. He said, "The computer is slave to the camera, because without a good photograph all the technology in the world doesn't take a good picture. You have to have a good photograph to begin with."

David LaChapelle uses photography to create surrealist images.

Quoted in designboom, "David LaChapelle: Interview with One of Photography's Brightest Stars." www.designboom.com/eng/interview/lachapelle.html.

on a piano decorated with leopard spots, surrounded by stuffed leopards in a room whose walls are adorned with huge depictions of bananas and cherries. Another image in the retrospective is *Parasol*, a fashion photo published in *Italian Vogue* in 2005. The shot features a beautiful model in a flowing white gown, carrying a torn umbrella and walking past a scene of devastation in which a home has been torn in two with debris scattered about the front lawn. Said the magazine,

> Desperate housewives are never more desperate than the ones in David LaChapelle's photographs. The image . . . part of a recent fashion story shot for *Italian Vogue,* has all the essential LaChapellian motifs: sex, chaos, humor, and a healthy disrespect for visual logic. When he looks at a suburban street, he sees a surreal landscape in which the quaint lives of soccer moms can be disrupted by sudden disaster, from a violent storm (in this case a hurricane) to the violent sexual yearnings caused by the sighting of a rock star. This elegant mom blithely walks away from the turbulence, strangely ambivalent to the uprooted world around her. Perhaps, like LaChapelle himself, she simply enjoys the spectacle of it all.[76]

Like most photographers working today, LaChapelle creates pictures through digital imaging, which has created many opportunities for the surrealist artist. Actually, anybody with access to a computer, the Internet, a digital camera, and a photo editing program can become a surrealist. The twenty-first-century surrealist artist can start by taking his or her own digital pictures. Then, with millions of images available on the Internet, the artist can find all manner of weird and bizarre images to download. Using the photo editing program, these shots of the familiar and unfamiliar can be chopped up and refashioned into surrealist art. It is likely that surrealism's first photographer, Man Ray, would approve of this technique. He once said, "I never think about art, and I don't think the old masters ever thought they were creating art. They had to express the spirit of their times. They would start to invent. And those were the Surrealists of their time. Every period had its Surrealists."[77]

Pop Surrealism

Of course, some surrealists prefer to do it the way that Dalí, Ernst, and Magritte created surrealism—with paint brushes and canvases. Many major cities feature at least one gallery that specializes in surrealist art produced by contemporary painters. So far none of these artists has attained the fame, wealth, and recognition of the original surrealists; nevertheless, a small and dedicated segment of the art-loving community maintains a fascination with the surrealist school. Although they may not have mastered the art of mining their own subconscious thoughts, there is no question that today's surrealist artists are producing some truly bizarre images that carry on the work of the original surrealist masters.

Today's surrealist artists have a new name for their genre: They call it "pop surrealism." It is also known as "lowbrow" art, but many pop surrealists regard that as a derogatory term. Pop surrealist art can be found in the pages of the quarterly journal *Juxtapoz*, a publication founded in 1994 by California artist Robert Williams. Pop surrealism often carries dark messages. While the characters are usually drawn as cartoonish figures, the messages and images are just as bizarre as those painted by Dalí, who serves as an icon to the movement. Said Williams, "When we started *Juxtapoz*, we wanted a place for the outlaw art that wasn't being seen anywhere."[78]

While the pop surrealists churn out their unique brand of surrealism, the paintings, photographs, films, and other works produced by the original artists from the 1920s and 1930s continue to draw large audiences. In recent years major surrealist shows featuring the works of Dalí, Man Ray, Ernst, and the other founders of the movement have been held at major museums in many large American cities. In 2005 an exhibition of Dalí's paintings at the Philadelphia Museum of Art drew tens of thousands of visitors. The curators of the show

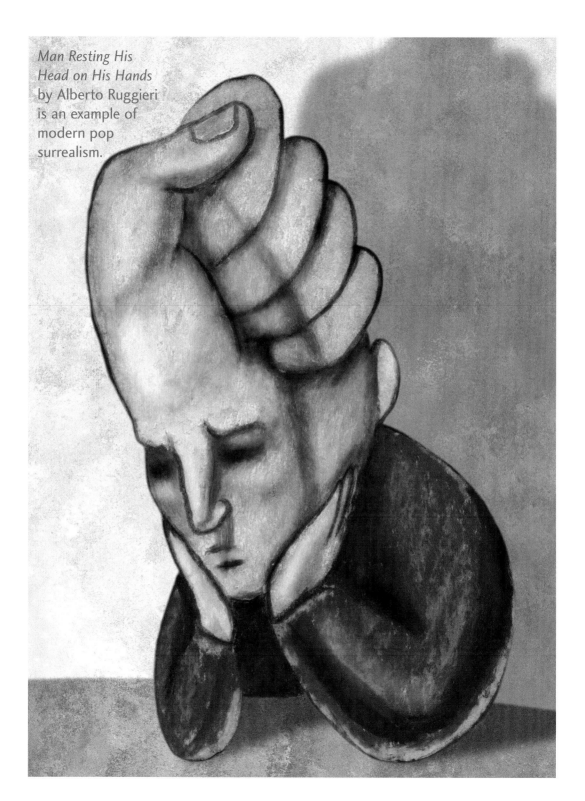

Man Resting His Head on His Hands by Alberto Ruggieri is an example of modern pop surrealism.

dedicated a large portion of the museum to the late Spanish surrealist's work. Some two hundred of his paintings were exhibited. In fact, the concrete steps to the museum—made famous by Sylvester Stallone in the boxing film *Rocky*—were decorated with a huge and colorful portrait of Dalí plastered right to the concrete surface, spanning thousands of square feet. Said Anne d'Harnoncourt, director of the museum, "Dalí is one of the best known artists of all time and yet, 16 years after his death and despite such remarkable public recognition, his achievement has yet to be fully understood. This exhibition will provide a splendid opportunity for scholars, artists, and visitors to encounter a complete and complex picture of the artist's oeuvre."[79]

The Dalí show proved to be highly successful; in fact, the museum was forced to extend the show by two weeks because of all the requests for tickets. Judging by the popularity of the exhibition, it is clear that the work of Dalí and his contemporaries still commands a dedicated audience. A large number of people have observed the original surrealist art work up close and have found themselves as confused and as captivated by the movement as the first audiences were more than three-quarters of a century ago.

Notes

Introduction: What Is Surrealism?

1. Tim Martin, *Essential Surrealists*. Bath, UK: Dempsey Parr, 1999, p. 6.
2. Quoted in Ritchie Robertson, "Are Freud's Dreams Coming True?" *Psychology Today*, January 2000, p. 50.
3. Jennifer Mundy, ed., *Surrealism: Desire Unbound*. Princeton, NJ: Princeton University Press, 2001, p. 12.
4. Quoted in Jonathan Lear, *Freud*. Oxford, UK: Routledge, 2005, p. 90.

Chapter 1: The Birth of Surrealism

5. Quoted in Hans Richter, *Dada: Art and Anti-Art*. New York: Thames and Hudson, 1997, p. 37.
6. Alfred H. Barr Jr., *Cubism and Abstract Art*. Cambridge, MA: Harvard University Press, 1986, p. 78.
7. Quoted in Martin Ries, "André Masson: Surrealism and His Discontents," *Art Journal*, Winter 2002, p. 74.
8. Quoted in René Passeron, *Surrealism*. Paris: Pierre Terrail, 2001, p. 15.
9. Quoted in Anna Balakian, *André Breton: Magus of Surrealism*. New York: Oxford University Press, 1971, p. 64.
10. André Breton, *Manifesto of Surrealism*, University of Alabama Department of Telecommunications and Film. www.tcf.ua.edu/Classes/Jbutler/T340/SurManifesto/ManifestoOfSurrealism.htm.
11. Breton, *Manifesto of Surrealism*.
12. Uwe M. Schneede, *Surrealism*. New York: Harry N. Abrams, 1972, p. 62.
13. Martin, *Essential Surrealists*, p. 79.
14. Carolyn Lanchner, *Joan Miró*. New York: Museum of Modern Art, 1993, p. 33.
15. Quoted in Schneede, *Surrealism*, p. 76.
16. A.M. Hammacher, *Magritte*. New York: Harry N. Abrams, 1985, p. 48.
17. Schneede, *Surrealism*, p. 104.
18. Quoted in Paul Moorehouse, *Dali*. San Diego: Thunder Bay, 1990, pp. 8–9.
19. Quoted in Schneede, *Surrealism*, p. 92.

Chapter 2: The Surrealists

20. Quoted in Moorehouse, *Dali*, p. 15.
21. Quoted in Moorehouse, *Dali*, p. 15.
22. Quoted in Robert Goff, *The Essential Salvador Dalí*. New York: Harry N. Abrams, 1998, p. 14.
23. Moorehouse, *Dali*, p. 92.
24. Goff, *The Essential Dalí*, p. 57.
25. Quoted in BBC, "Influences in the

Life of Salvador Dalí," July 6, 2001. www.bbc.co.uk/dna/h2g2/A585344.

26. Quoted in BBC, "Influences in the Life of Salvador Dalí."

27. Ingrid Schaffner, *The Essential Man Ray*. New York: Harry N. Abrams, 2003, p. 34.

28. Quoted in *American Masters*, "Man Ray," PBS. www.pbs.org/wnet/amer icanmasters/database/ray_m.html.

29. Marina Vanci-Perahim, *Man Ray*. New York: Harry N. Abrams, 1998, p. 56.

30. Schaffner, *The Essential Man Ray*, p. 27.

31. David Sylvester, *Magritte: The Silence of the Word*. New York: Harry N. Abrams, 1992, p. 296.

32. Bradley Collins Jr., "Psychoanalysis and Art History," *Art Journal*, Summer 1990, p. 182.

33. José María Faerna, *Ernst*. New York: Harry N. Abrams, 1997, p. 21.

34. John Russell, *Max Ernst: Life and Work*. New York: Harry N. Abrams, 1967, p. 133.

35. Jacques Lassaigne, *Miró*. Paris: Editions d'Art, 1963, p. 40.

36. Lassaigne, *Miró*, p. 41.

37. Schneede, *Surrealism*, p. 86.

Chapter 3: The Surrealists' Influences

38. Schneede, *Surrealism*, p. 51.

39. Quoted in Patrick Waldberg, *Surrealism*. London: Thames and Hudson, 1997, p. 28.

40. *Time*, "Marvelous and Fantastic,"
December 14, 1936, p. 60.

41. Quoted in Steven Naifeh and Gregory White Smith, *Jackson Pollock: An American Saga*. New York: Clarkson N. Potter, 1989, p. 417.

42. Quoted in Naifeh and Smith, *Jackson Pollock*, p. 419.

43. Quoted in Naifeh and Smith, *Jackson Pollock*, p. 454.

44. Schneede, *Surrealism*, p. 132.

45. Quoted in Mundy, *Surrealism: Desire Unbound*, p. 197.

46. Mariann Smith, "*Sunrise* 1954–1955," Albright-Knox Art Gallery. www.al brightknox.org/ArtStart/Hare.html.

47. Quoted in Victor Bockris, *The Life and Death of Andy Warhol*. New York: Bantam, 1989, p. 151.

48. Bruce H. Hinrich, "Chaos and Cosmos: The Search for Meaning in Modern Art," *Humanist*, March/April 1995, p. 22.

49. Quoted in Bob Colacello, *Holy Terror: Andy Warhol Close Up*. New York: HarperCollins, 1990, p. 175.

50. Hayden Herrera, *Frida Kahlo: The Paintings*. New York: Perennial, 1991, pp. 188–90.

51. Quoted in Mundy, *Surrealism: Desire Unbound*, p. 201.

52. Quoted in Mundy, *Surrealism: Desire Unbound*, p. 201.

53. Quoted in Mundy, *Surrealism: Desire Unbound*, p. 198.

Chapter 4: Surrealism and Social Change

54. André Breton, *Conversations: The Au-*

tobiography of Surrealism. New York: Paragon House, 1993, p. 97.

55. Quoted in Charles Harrison and Paul Wood, eds., *Art in Theory 1900–2000: An Anthology of Changing Ideas.* Malden, MA: Blackwell, 2003, p. 534.

56. Quoted in Manny Thain, "Real Enough," *Socialism Today,* October 2001. www.socialismtoday.org/60/surrealism/html.

57. H.H. Arnason, Marla F. Prather, and Daniel Wheeler, *History of Modern Art.* New York: Harry N. Abrams, 1998, p. 286.

58. Hammacher, *Magritte,* p. 86.

59. Quoted in Moorehouse, *Dali,* p. 82.

60. Goff, *The Essential Salvador Dalí,* p. 69.

61. Quoted in Martin, *Essential Surrealists,* p. 136.

62. Moorehouse, *Dali,* p. 94.

63. Faerna, *Ernst,* p. 50.

64. Quoted in Richard Lacayo, "Dalí Goes to Rehab," *Time,* February 21, 2005, p. 59.

65. Quoted in Stanley Meisler, "The Surreal World of Salvador Dalí," *Smithsonian,* April 2005, p. 72.

66. Quoted in Andrew Hussey, "Brit Art's Original Bad Boy," *Times of London,* July 21, 2001.

67. Tate Gallery, *"The Change."* www.tate.org/servlet/ViewWork?wordid=17344.

68. Quoted in *Times of London,* "Ralph Rumney," March 29, 2002.

69. Quoted in Situationist International Online, "Slogans to Be Spread Now by Every Means," Virginia Tech University. www.cddc.vt.edu/sionline/si/slogans.html.

70. Walter Erben, *Joan Miró: The Man and His Work.* Cologne, Ger.: Benedikt Taschen, 1998, p. 208.

Chapter 5: Surrealism Today

71. Jack Matthews, "Mysterious as *Velvet,* David Lynch Regains Form in *Lost Highway,*" *Newsday,* February 21, 1997, p. B-13.

72. Ian Johns, "Here's One in the Eye," *Times of London,* September 19, 2001.

73. Bettina L. Knapp, *Jean Cocteau.* New York: Twayne, 1970, pp. 140–41.

74. Johns, "Here's One in the Eye."

75. Wesley Morris, "Now That's What I Call Video," *Boston Globe,* February 5, 2006, p. N-11.

76. Jeffrey Elbies, "Weird World: A Mammoth New Collector's Edition Book Puts David LaChapelle's Astonishing Career in Perspective," *American Photo,* July/August 2006, p. 32.

77. Quoted in *Morning Edition,* "Profile: New Surrealist Art Exhibition at the Metropolitan Museum of Art in New York," National Public Radio, March 5, 2002.

78. Quoted in Doug Harvey, "Pictures from the Unibrow Revolution," *L.A. Weekly,* October 27, 2005. www.laweekly.com/general/features/pictures-from-the-unibrowrevolution/179.

79. Quoted in "The Grand Master of Surrealism: Salvador Dalí," *USA Today Magazine,* May 2005, p. 34.

For More Information

Books

Ruth Brandon, *Surreal Lives: The Surrealists, 1917–1945*. New York: Grove, 1999. The story of how surrealism grew among the poets, writers, and artists who congregated in Paris following World War I.

José María Faerna, ed., *Ernst*. New York: Harry N. Abrams, 1997. Large coffee table–style book includes dozens of color reprints of the artist's work as well as interpretations of his paintings. The book includes a brief biography of the artist.

Robert Goff, *The Essential Salvador Dalí*. New York: Harry N. Abrams, 1998. A thorough biography of the artist, including reprints of his work and photographs of the artist in some of his most flamboyant moments.

Tim Martin, *Essential Surrealists*. Bath, UK: Dempsey Parr, 1999. Picture-by-picture interpretation of some of the genre's most important painters, including Ernst, Dalí, Masson, Miró, Man Ray, and Magritte. Other artists whose works are analyzed are Picasso, Duchamp, and Pollock.

Paul Moorehouse, *Dali*. San Diego: Thunder Bay, 1990. The coffee table book includes a biography of the artist as well as interpretations of dozens of Dalí's most familiar works.

Jennifer Mundy, ed., *Surrealism: Desire Unbound*. Princeton, NJ: Princeton University Press, 2001. The book was published as a companion volume to an extensive surrealism exhibition at London's Tate Gallery in 2001 and 2002; it includes reprints of hundreds of works of surrealism as well as essays on the genre written by some of the world's leading art critics.

Steven Naifeh and Gregory White Smith, *Jackson Pollock: An American Saga*. New York: Clarkson N. Potter, 1989. The biography of the abstract expressionist includes a lengthy chapter on Pollock's introduction to surrealism and how he was influenced by the genre.

René Passeron, *Surrealism*. Paris: Pierre Terrail, 2001. A history of surrealism told through the author's interpretations of dozens of paintings by the movement's most familiar artists; includes a chapter on the political messages contained in surrealist art.

Hans Richter, *Dada: Art and Anti-Art*. New York: Thames and Hudson,

1997. The story of how the movement grew in Europe and how such Dada artists as Duchamp and Arp developed the genre.

Martica Sawin, *Surrealism in Exile and the Beginning of the New York School.* Cambridge, MA: MIT Press, 1995. Concentrates on the surrealists who arrived in America in the 1930s and how they influenced American abstract artists.

Uwe M. Schneede, *Surrealism.* New York: Harry N. Abrams, 1972. The book includes in-depth interpretations of surrealist art as well as a history of the surrealist and Dada movements by a noted German art critic and museum director.

Patrick Waldberg, *Surrealism.* London: Thames and Hudson, 1997. History of the surrealism movement; readers will find dozens of photographs of the surrealists during their most productive years in the 1920s and 1930s.

Periodicals

Jeffrey Elbies, "Weird World: A Mammoth New Collector's Edition Book Puts David LaChapelle's Astonishing Career in Perspective," *American Photo*, July/August 2006. The surrealist photographer's work is examined in a lengthy retrospective.

Stanley Meisler, "The Surreal World of Salvador Dalí," *Smithsonian*, April 2005. Examination of Dalí's life written during a major exhibit of the surrealist's work at the Philadelphia Museum of Art.

Martin Ries, "André Masson: Surrealism and His Discontents," *Art Journal*, Winter 2002. A biographical sketch of the artist, who first felt the spark of surrealism while lying gravely wounded on a World War I battlefield.

Time, "Marvelous and Fantastic," December 14, 1936. *Time*'s original story on the invasion of the surrealists may be available on microfilm at a public library; the story concentrates on the weird and flamboyant world of surrealist artists, indicating that back in 1936 Americans did not know quite what to make of them.

Web Sites

American Masters: "ManRay" (www.pbs.org/wnet/americanmas ters/data base/ray_m.html). Companion Web site to the PBS documentary on the American surrealist painter and photographer; includes a biography of Man Ray, examples of his work, and a lengthy chronology of his life.

André Breton, *Manifesto of Surrealism* (www.tcf.ua.edu/Classes/Jbut ler/T340/SurManifesto/Manifesto OfSurrealism.htm). Breton's manifesto can be read in its entirety on this Web site maintained by the University of Alabama Department of Telecommunications and Film.

Juxtapoz (www.juxtapoz.com/jux). The quarterly journal of pop surrealism includes many images of surrealist art rendered by contemporary artists.

The site also includes a list of exhibitions and other events involving pop surrealism, articles on pop surrealism and reviews of recent work, and a page where readers can post their own art.

Salvador Dalí Museum (www.salvadordalimuseum.org/home.html). The Web site for the museum in St. Petersburg, Florida, includes many resources for the student studying the Spanish surrealist, including a biography of Dalí, online videos featuring curators discussing Dalí's work, and instructions for students on how to make their own Dalí "characters," including his long-legged elephants and giraffes.

Situationist International Online (www.cddc.vt.edu/sionline). A history of the situationist movement can be found on this Web site maintained by Virginia Tech University. The student can find an archive of essays, letters, and other writings by prominent situationists; a chronology of events, bibliography of books, and other resources; and links to other Web sites that examine situationism.

Surrealist Movement of the United States (www.surrealistmovement-usa.org). The organization's Web site features examples of art produced by contemporary artists as well as poetry, reviews of literature, and essays about surrealist thought.

Index

Russia, 64

sand pictures, 45–46
Satie, Erik, 11
Schaffner, Ingrid, 38, 40
Schneede, Uwe M.
    on development of
        surrealism, 47
    on *Elephant of Celebes*, 23–24
    on *Menaced Assassin, The*, 27
    on sand pictures by Masson,
        46
    on work of Tanning, 54
Scream, The (Picasso), 49–50
sculpture, 38, 54, 56
She-Wolf (Pollock), 53
situationism, 75–76, 77–78
sleep
    deprivation, 43, 45
    subconscious during, 12, 13
Smith, Mariann, 54, 56
socialism
    Breton and, 20, 63–64
    Dalí and, 34
    fascism in Spain and, 67–70
    Grosz and, 66, 67
    Man Ray and, 65
    philosophy, 64–65, 87
    Situationist International, 75
*Soft Construction with Boiled
    Beans—Premonition of Civil
    War* (Dalí), 68–69
solarization process, 40
Soupault, Philippe, 19, 21
Spanish Civil War, 67–70
Spellbound (film), 85
Spiegel, Adam. *See* Jonze,
    Spike
Still Life with Playing Cards
    (Braque), 18
subconscious

Dalí and, 29
    importance of, 12–13
    literature and, 15
    Masson and, 45–46
    Miró and, 24, 43
Sunrise (Hare), 54, 56
surrealism
    background of, 12–13, 16,
        17, 18, 20
    defined, 10-11, 21
    first coined, 12, 26
    goal, 14
    influence of
        on films, 26, 81–87
        on Kahlo, 59–60, 62
        on music videos, 87–88, 89
        on Picasso, 49–50
        on pop art, 47, 56–59
        on pop surrealism, 91, 93
        on situationism, 75–76
        on television, 79–81, 84
    rules of, 19, 21–22
Swan Lake (ballet) on
    television, 84
Swiss surrealists, 27
Sylvester, David, 41
symbolist literature, 20
synthetic cubism, 16, 18

Tanning, Dorothea, 53–54, 73
techniques
    adopted from cubism, 18
    blotted, 57, 59
    decalcomania, 42–43, 57, 73
    frottage, 42
    photographic, 40, 90–91
    simple objects representing
        complex thoughts, 24
television, 79–81, 87–88
Temptations of St. Anthony, The
    (Ernst), 73

themes
    images within images, 35
    merger of real with unreal,
        23–24, 31, 54, 56
    space as dreamscapes,
        38–39
    time, 37
    unusual as part of everyday
        life, 12, 34
There Is No Finished World
    (Masson), 72
Time (magazine)
    Art of This Century gallery,
        52
    Dalí, 30, 58
    Museum of Modern Art
        exhibition, 50
Times of London (newspaper),
    82
Towards a Revolutionary Art
    (Trotsky, Breton and Rivera),
    64
Trotsky, Leon, 64, 66

Underground Figure (Masson),
    24
U.S. Postal Service stamps,
    17

Vanci-Perahim, Marina, 39
Venice, Italy, 76
Violon d'Ingres, Le (*Violin of
    Ingress, The* by Man Ray),
    40
VVV (journal), 56

Warhol, Andy, 47, 56–59, 89
Wheeler, Daniel, 66, 67
Williams, Robert, 91
World War I, 19, 46
World War II, 43, 64, 70, 72

About the Author

Hal Marcovitz has written nearly one hundred books for young readers. His other books in the Eye on Art series include *Anime*, *Computer Animation*, and *Art Conservation*. He lives in Chalfont, Pennsylvania, with his wife Gail and daughters Michelle and Ashley.